Sumerian Mythology

Captivating Myths of Gods, Goddesses, and Legendary Creatures of Ancient Sumer and Their Importance to the Sumerians

© Copyright 2019

All Rights Reserved. No part of this book may be reproduced in any form without permission in writing from the author. Reviewers may quote brief passages in reviews.

Disclaimer: No part of this publication may be reproduced or transmitted in any form or by any means, mechanical or electronic, including photocopying or recording, or by any information storage and retrieval system, or transmitted by email without permission in writing from the publisher.

While all attempts have been made to verify the information provided in this publication, neither the author nor the publisher assumes any responsibility for errors, omissions or contrary interpretations of the subject matter herein.

This book is for entertainment purposes only. The views expressed are those of the author alone, and should not be taken as expert instruction or commands. The reader is responsible for his or her own actions.

Adherence to all applicable laws and regulations, including international, federal, state and local laws governing professional licensing, business practices, advertising and all other aspects of doing business in the US, Canada, UK or any other jurisdiction is the sole responsibility of the purchaser or reader.

Neither the author nor the publisher assumes any responsibility or liability whatsoever on the behalf of the purchaser or reader of these materials. Any perceived slight of any individual or organization is purely unintentional.

Free Bonus from Captivating History (Available for a Limited time)

Hi History Lovers!

Now you have a chance to join our exclusive history list so you can get your first history ebook for free as well as discounts and a potential to get more history books for free! Simply visit the link below to join.

Captivatinghistory.com/ebook

Also, make sure to follow us on Facebook, Twitter and Youtube by searching for Captivating History.

Contents

INTRODUCTION 1
PART I: TALES OF GODS AND GODDESSES 5
ENKI AND NINMAH 5
ENLIL AND NINLIL 8
ENKI AND NINHURSAG 12
THE EXPLOITS OF NINURTA 19
THE JOURNEY OF NANNA TO NIPPUR 26
INANNA AND EBIH 30
DUMUZI AND ENKIMDU 34
THE MARRIAGE OF MARTU 36
PART II: TALES OF KINGS AND HEROES 40
ENMERKAR AND THE ENSUHKESHDANNA 40
LUGALBANDA IN THE MOUNTAIN CAVE 45
LUGALBANDA AND THE ANZU BIRD 50
THE SUMERIAN GILGAMESH 57
PART I: INANNA AND THE HULUPPU TREE 57

PART II: ENKIDU IN THE UNDERWORLD	60
PART III: GILGAMESH AND HUWAWA	66
PART IV: GILGAMESH AND AGA	74
BIBLIOGRAPHY	84
GLOSSARY	87

Introduction

Sumerian literature comprises one of the oldest collections of written documents in the world. Like other bodies of mythology created by myriad cultures, the Sumerian corpus contains stories explaining the origins of the world, myths of the deeds and foibles of all-too-human deities and semi-divine beings, tales of magic and miracles, and epics detailing the mighty exploits of heroes who by their great strength and skill overcome dangerous beasts and human enemies alike. Surviving texts in Sumerian also include a number of religious texts composed by Enheduanna, the daughter of Sargon of Akkad and the high priestess in the temple of the moon god Nanna, as well as the first named author in human history.

The writing system used to record Sumerian texts of all kinds is known as cuneiform, for its use of a wedge-shaped stylus to make symbols impressed into soft clay tablets that were then left to dry, or were sometimes fired in a kiln, to preserve the writing. (The word "cuneiform" has its roots in the Latin word *cuneus*, meaning "wedge.") This system, thought to be the oldest form of writing in the world, was later adapted throughout Mesopotamia by speakers of languages such as Akkadian and Old Persian. Although an untold number of these tablets have been entirely lost, thousands of them have survived into the present day. However, many of the surviving tablets have come down to us broken and therefore incomplete, leading to difficulties in translating and reconstructing the texts that first began to be written down almost five thousand years ago.

The ancient Sumerian civilization began in the so-called "Fertile Crescent," an area around and between the Tigris and Euphrates Rivers in what is now Iraq. Starting around 3000 BCE, the Sumerians occupied the southern end of this Crescent, near the mouths of the rivers and not far from the Persian Gulf. The Sumerian people were among the first in the region to practice agriculture and to create city-states. They pioneered many important techniques in metalworking, the creation of textiles, and animal husbandry, and with their invention of cuneiform writing, they not only inscribed their religious texts but also kept very meticulous records of their business dealings and created the first corpus of written law.

Sumerian is what is known as a "language isolate," meaning that it appears to have no relationship to any other languages. Sometime around 2000 BCE, Sumerian fell out of use as a spoken tongue and was replaced as a vernacular by Akkadian (a Semitic language related to modern Amharic and Arabic); however, Sumerian remained as an elite literary and ritual language for many centuries afterward. One outcome of these shifts in language use is that Sumerian texts were recorded in both monolingual Sumerian forms and also in bilingual forms alongside the Akkadian versions.

Defining what constitutes "Sumerian" myth is complicated not only by the linguistic situation but by other historical events and cultural realities. Sumer was absorbed into the Akkadian Empire in 2234 BCE, and there is a generous amount of overlap between Sumerian and Akkadian religions and mythography that can make it difficult to disentangle one from the other. Therefore, for the purposes of this book, I have followed the lists and categorization of narratives provided in the Electronic Text Corpus of Sumerian Literature (ETCSL) created by the Faculty of Oriental Studies at the University of Oxford.

The myths presented in the present volume include tales of gods and goddesses, both major and minor, as well as kings and heroes, both historical and mythical. One such king is the hero of what many scholars believe to be the first written epic: Gilgamesh. Stories about Gilgamesh—a historical Sumerian king who later became deified and mythologized—and about his illustrious (and likely mythical) forbears, Lugalbanda and Enmerkar, form an important subset of the narratives recorded in the Sumerian language, and the Sumerian myths formed the basis for the expanded Akkadian epic best known to modern readers. The tale about Sargon of Akkad is also about an actual historical figure, although one for whom we have more reliable evidence than we do for Gilgamesh. However, the events related in the story that explains how Sargon rose to kingship have been mythologized, likely as part of an attempt to provide Sargon's reign with political and religious legitimacy.

Just as the stories of Gilgamesh are set in places that are at once historical and mythical, so, too, do the tales of the gods create an overlap between the physical world and the world of myth. In Sumerian myths, Enlil lives in his house, the E-kur, in the Sumerian city of Nippur, but this is not merely a mythical house populated by mythical beings: The E-kur was the actual structure made by Sumerians as a temple for the worship of Enlil. And just as historical, physical Nippur was a place of pilgrimage in actuality, it also is in myth, as we see in the story of Nanna's journey to that city to visit his divine father, Enlil.

In addition to creating connections between the human world and the divine, Sumerian myths explain how the world came to be in the first place. These myths establish the cosmic order, which places the greater gods, or Annunaki, at the top of the hierarchy, with the lesser gods, or Igigi, below them. Below the Igigi are human beings, who, according to the Sumerians, were created to do the work of building and farming that the Igigi originally had been assigned to do, thus making human beings responsible not only for their own sustenance but for that of the gods. Other stories tell how some of the lesser deities came to be, often as the result of both rape and incest. We see this in the story of Enki and Ninhursag, for example.

Heroic strength capable of bringing mountains to their knees is the province of both male and female deities in Sumerian myth. The god Ninurta does battle with the evil Asag and rearranges the mountains to allow the Tigris and Euphrates to flow, while the goddess Inanna brings down Mount Ebih in revenge for the mountain's refusal to do the goddess reverence.

Less lofty human concerns are also encapsulated in two other myths that explain something about the interactions of differing cultures. The story of Dumuzi and Enkimdu is a mythologized version of the potential conflicts between pastoral and agricultural peoples, while the story of Martu's marriage explains the merging of the nomadic Amorite people with more settled, urbanized cultures.

The original Sumerian texts of these stories are poetic in nature and often contain a significant number of repeated phrases. For the purposes of this book, I have rendered the stories in prose and have smoothed out the repetitions in order to make the language flow as such. I have also included a glossary of names and places for modern readers who may not be familiar with Sumerian mythography. But however these stories are transmitted, they will always tell us how this ancient people understood their world and their place in it, as well as about the customs and relationships they found to be most important.

Part I: Tales of Gods and Goddesses

Enki and Ninmah

This creation myth is both unusual and important in that it deals not only with the establishment of cosmic order and how humanity came to be but also directly with the issue of human disability. Here Enki challenges Ninmah (the mother goddess also known as Ninhursag) to create a being with a flaw that cannot be fixed, but each time Ninmah presents Enki with one of her disabled creations, Enki decrees a place for them in society. After Ninmah makes several attempts to best Enki and fails, Enki declares it to be his turn to create something. When Enki creates a being that is so disabled that Ninmah cannot find a solution, the contest comes to an end, although the final portion of the story is fragmented, and it is unclear exactly what happens to Enki's creation or how Enki's apparent victory over Ninmah is decided.

In her dictionary of Near Eastern mythology, Assyriologist Gwendolyn Leick has a somewhat different interpretation for the character of Umul, the creature made by Enki. Based on the list of Umul's characteristics, Leick suggests that rather than being a severely disabled adult, this creature is, in fact, the first baby.

When the heavens and the Earth were first created, there were only the gods and goddesses to dwell in it. The goddesses became the wives of the gods, and the gods did the work of fashioning the Earth. The Annunaki acted as planners and supervisors, determining what was to be done. The Igigi did the labor according to the Annunakis' commands. The Igigi dug the beds of the rivers, they heaped up the mountains. It was ponderous toil, and the Igigi were discontented.

While that work was going on, Enki, the god of wisdom, had retired to his chamber in the Apsu, where he took his rest. As the Annunaki planned and the Igigi toiled, Enki slept. The Igigi said amongst themselves, "It is Enki's fault that we must labor like this." But Enki slept on and did not hear their complaints.

Finally, Namma, great mother of the gods, went to Enki and woke him. "Arise from your bed, Enki. The gods are discontented with their labors and have begun to rebel. Arise from your bed, and help them. Create a substitute for them, one who can do this labor in their stead."

Enki arose from his bed and went to his council chamber, where he thought long about what should be done. Finally, he created two birth-goddesses. Then he summoned his mother Namma and said, "Take you a measure of clay and mix it with drops of my blood. When it is well mixed, cut it into portions, and with the help of your fellow goddesses, shape the pieces of clay into beings."

And so it was that Enki and the goddesses created men and women. The new beings were given life, and when the men and women saw one another, they desired to be married. Each man married one of the women, and soon they were having children of their own. Enki and the goddesses placed the new beings on the Earth and gave to them the labors that the Igigi had done before. Relieved of their tasks, the gods fell at Enki's feet and praised him for his wisdom. Then they declared a great feast to celebrate the works of Enki.

At the feast, Enki and Ninmah drank beer together. Ninmah said to Enki, "I have the power to decree the fate of human beings. I can make their bodies well or ill. This is a power I hold."

Enki answered, "Well, then, whatever fate or fashion you decree for human beings, I can change it to its opposite."

So, Ninmah took a piece of clay and fashioned it into a man with weak, withered hands that could not grasp anything. Enki looked upon him and decreed that he should be a servant to the king.

Ninmah took another piece of clay and fashioned it into a blind man. Enki gave to the blind man the gift of music and set him to sing in the presence of the king.

A third man Ninmah made, one with malformed feet. Enki gave the man with malformed feet the gift of silversmithing and set him to work making beautiful things for the king.

Then Ninmah made an incontinent man, whose urine constantly leaked from his body. Enki took the man and bathed him in water that he had blessed, and the man was cured.

Ninmah made a woman who could not bear children. Enki gave to the woman the gift of weaving and sent her to make beautiful cloth in the house of the queen.

Another person Ninmah made, one that was neither male nor female. Enki decreed that this being should be called a eunuch and that they should work as a servant in the household of the king.

Ninmah was wroth, for Enki had bested her every time. She took the last remaining piece of clay and threw it to the floor. The gods saw this, and the feasting chamber fell silent.

"You have made six beings, and I have given them gifts that they might live," said Enki. "Come now, let me create a being, and you must decree its fate."

Enki created a new being, and it was called Umul. It was weak and shriveled. All its ribs were showing. It could not hold up its head. It could neither walk nor speak. It could neither eat nor drink. Then Enki said to Ninmah, "I gave gifts to all of your creatures that they might live; now you must do the same for mine."

Ninmah went to Umul and spoke to him, but he did not answer. She offered him food, but he could not take it. She tried to help him stand, she tried to help him sit, but Umul could not do those things.

Ninmah went to Enki and said, "I do not know what to do. This being seems to be neither alive nor dead. Certainly he cannot work and will not be able to support himself."

Enki replied, "Come now. For each flawed being you created, I decreed a fate. I gave each one a gift."

[The remainder of the story is fragmented, but the surviving pieces seem to indicate that Enki won the competition. It is unclear exactly what fate was ultimately decreed for Umul, although in W. G. Lambert's translation, Enki says of Umul, "May he make my house."]

Enlil and Ninlil

Enlil was the primary god of the Sumerian pantheon. The main cult center for his worship was in the city of Nippur, where the temple dedicated to him was known as the E-kur. Enlil was the firstborn son of the great god An, and as such, he was usually thought of as a god who dispensed judgements and decreed fates. He is often associated with wind and air, and he was thought to bring both prosperity and calamity alike.

Ninlil was the consort of Enlil, and her name is actually an honorific referencing her husband's name. One version of the story of the wedding of Enlil and Ninlil states that Ninlil's name originally was Sud and that she received her new name when she married Enlil.

The primary function of the myth of Enlil and Ninlil is to explain the origins of Nanna, Nergal, Ninazu, and Enbilulu, the gods of the moon, of war and the Underworld, of boundaries, and of canals, respectively. It also positions Ninlil as a mother goddess. But as scholar Gwendolyn Leick observes in her book about the sexual and erotic aspects of Mesopotamian literature, we also can see some of the values that ancient peoples placed upon social standards for young men and women when they came of age to have children together. Leick notes that Enlil is cast out of the Ki-ur because he has had intercourse with Ninlil before marrying her.

Although we know what the E-kur was and what it was for in both its physical manifestation in ancient Nippur and in its mythical sense, the meaning of "Ki-ur" remains obscure. Assyriologist Samuel Kramer discusses the word in some footnotes to his article on the Sumerian flood myth where he suggests that it means something like "countryside," apparently referring to rural areas that, while inhabited, exist in opposition to populous cities. In the myth of Enlil and Ninlil, the "Ki-ur" appears to refer to some sort of place where the gods reside, a place that is both outside the city and that requires those who enter it to be ritually pure.

Once in the city of Nippur, there lived a young woman named Ninlil and a young man named Enlil. The young woman was very beautiful, and the young man was strong and brave. Ninlil lived with her mother, a wise old woman named Nunbarshegunu. Now, there was nothing that Ninlil liked better than to go down to the river and stroll along its banks. But Nunbarshegunu did not want her daughter to go down to the river because the young Enlil also liked to walk along the riverbanks and sail on the water.

"Stay away from the river," said Nunbarshegunu, "and you must never bathe in it! That young Enlil is always there. What if he sees you walking along the holy river or bathing in it? What if he sees you and desires you, and what if he has his way with you? What will you do then?"

Ninlil did not listen to her mother. Every day, she went down to the river and walked along its banks. One day, Enlil happened to be at the river at the same time as Ninlil. Enlil saw how beautiful Ninlil was, and he was entranced. Enlil went up to Ninlil and said, "You are so beautiful! Please let me kiss you, let me lie with you! Do not turn me away, for I love you!"

But Ninlil would not let Enlil lie with her. She said, "I am too young to kiss any man and certainly too young to lie with him. What if you get me with child? What will I do then? Besides, if my mother and father found out what we had done, they would be wroth with me."

And so, Ninlil went away, and Enlil did not get his desire.

Enlil did not know what to do next, so he went to speak to Nuska, the Master Builder of the E-kur, the House of the Gods. "Nuska," said Enlil, "do you know that young woman who walks along the river every day? Her name is Ninlil, and she is very beautiful. Tell me, does she have any other suitors? Has anyone ever kissed her before?"

For answer, Nuska said, "Get into my boat, O Enlil, and I will take you to her." Nuska sailed them down the river, and all along the way, Enlil thought to himself how delightful it would be to finally kiss Ninlil and to finally lie together.

Soon enough, Enlil found Ninlil. He kissed her and poured his seed into her womb, and Ninlil was got with child. And thus it was that Ninlil bore Nanna, the god of the moon.

Then Enlil went to the Ki-ur for he had a mind to wander about there. But the gods had seen what he had done with Ninlil, and they had him arrested. The gods told Enlil that for his deed he was to be cast out of the city for he was now impure.

Enlil went to the gates to leave the city. Ninlil saw him go and followed behind him. Enlil knew that Ninlil was there and did not want Ninlil to follow him. He did not want her to know where he was going. When Enlil arrived at the city gates, he went to the gatekeeper and said, "Do you see the beautiful Ninlil who follows me? If she asks where I have gone, you must tell her that you do not know."

Ninlil arrived at the gate. She asked the gatekeeper where Enlil had gone. But the gatekeeper was not there; Enlil had taken his form and taken his place. In the form of the gatekeeper, Enlil said, "I have not seen him at all, my lady. I do not know where he is."

"Well," said Ninlil, "if that is the case, then you must come and lie with me once I have had my child. For this is Enlil's child, and since he is your lord, that makes me your lady."

The gatekeeper and Ninlil lay together and delighted in one another. Enlil poured his seed into her womb, and Ninlil was got with child. And thus it was that Ninlil bore Nergal, the god of war and the Underworld.

Then Enlil went to the Id-kura, the river that flows between the land of the living and the Underworld, and Ninlil followed him. Enlil went to the man who dwelt beside the Id-kura and said, "Do you see the beautiful Ninlil who follows me? If she asks where I have gone, you must tell her that you do not know."

Ninlil arrived at the river. She asked the man who dwelt beside the river where Enlil had gone. But the man was not there; Enlil had taken his form and taken his place. In the form of the man who dwelt by the Id-kura, Enlil said, "I have not seen him at all, my lady. I do not know where he is."

"Well," said Ninlil, "if that is the case, then you must come and lie with me once I have had my child. For this is Enlil's child, and since he is your lord, that makes me your lady."

The man who dwelt by the Id-kura and Ninlil lay together and delighted in one another. Enlil poured his seed into her womb, and Ninlil became heavy with child. And thus it was that Ninlil bore Ninazu, the god who sets the boundaries of the fields.

Then Enlil left Ninlil and went walking along the river, and Ninlil followed him. Enlil went to the ferryman and said, "Do you see the beautiful Ninlil who follows me? If she asks where I have gone, you must tell her that you do not know."

Ninlil arrived at the river. She asked the ferryman where Enlil had gone. But the man was not there; Enlil had taken his form and taken his place. In the form of the ferryman, Enlil said, "I have not seen him at all, my lady. I do not know where he is."

"Well," said Ninlil, "if that is the case, then you must come and lie with me once I have had my child. For this is Enlil's child, and since he is your lord, that makes me your lady."

The ferryman and Ninlil lay together and delighted in one another. Enlil poured the seed of Enbilulu into her womb, and Ninlil was got with child. And thus it was that Ninlil bore Enbilulu, the god of canals.

Enki and Ninhursag

This story is set in the land of Dilmun, a place that is synonymous with peace and plenty in Sumerian literature. An actual historical Dilmun did exist; scholars have located it on the eastern side of the Arabian Peninsula along the Persian Gulf. Dilmun likely included what is now the island nation of Bahrain and the peninsula that is now the state of Qatar, and it was an important trading partner for Mesopotamian peoples. Over time, however, Dilmun became mythologized in Sumerian literature as a kind of paradise where there was neither sickness nor violence.

Enki, one of the main characters in this myth, is a creator god, a trickster, and is particularly associated with water. Enki also seems to have been conceived of as a sort of opposite to Enlil. In her dictionary of Near Eastern myth, Assyriologist Gwendolyn Leick notes that the name Enlil may be translated as "Lord Air," while Enki can be rendered as "Lord Earth." Whereas Enlil's primary cult center was in Nippur, Enki's main temple was in Eridu, a city in what is now south-central Iraq, to the west of the Euphrates River.

"Ninhursag" is but one of the many names of the Sumerian great mother goddess. Ninhursag is particularly associated with Enki, and according to Leick, the goddess' name is actually a title meaning

something like "Lady of the Wild Hills," a name that is given to her by her heroic son, Ninurta, in the myth of his battle against the evil Asag creature.

This story explains the origins of several lesser deities. First are Ninsar, Ninkura, and Uttu, who were associated with plants, mountain pastures, and weaving, respectively. As is common in ancient mythology, divine beings in Sumerian tales are often the products of incestuous relations, and this story participates in that tradition. Enki first has relations with Ninhursag and then with Ninsar, the daughter who is produced by that union, and then with her daughter Ninkura, and so on, until the fourth generation is reached with Uttu, whereupon Ninhursag puts a stop to the pattern by removing Enki's seed from her great-granddaughter's womb and uses it to create plants instead. When Enki consumes the plants without asking, Ninhursag departs in a rage and does not come back until a fox is sent by the Annunaki to fetch her. The story ends with Ninhursag healing Enki from the illness caused by her absence, and several more minor deities are named and possibly created in the process.

The original tablets containing this story are broken in places, as is common with these very ancient and very fragile documents. In some places it is possible to imagine what might have transpired in the parts of the story that are missing based on context, when there is enough material to make a guess at what happened. However, the portion of the story that shows how the fox brought Ninhursag back to the Annunaki is too scantily preserved to be recreated with any accuracy. I have noted this in the text of the myth at the appropriate point. Likewise, in the section where Ninhursag heals an ailing Enki piece by piece, some of the words for the affected body parts are missing or untranslatable and cannot be guessed from context. I have therefore replaced these with ellipses.

Far, far away, there is a land called Dilmun. Dilmun is a pure land, a land of peace and of plenty. Beasts of prey hunt not, carrion birds feed not. In Dilmun there is no sickness and no fear, there is no slow decline into agedness, and there is no death and no mourning. Toil and travail are known not. All is young, all is peaceful, all is pure, and there in that land of Dilmun did Enki lie with his consort in great joy.

One day, Ninsikila went to her father Enki and said, "O my father, all is well in Dilmun, all is peaceful and pure, but our city has no water. We have no river upon which to build a quay or sail boats. We have no canals to water our fields. There are no ponds that the beasts may drink from. Our wells are dry, and the people have nothing to drink. Give to us water, that we might live."

Enki thought upon Ninsikila's request and said, "When Utu the sun god appears in the sky, then shall Dilmun have water."

And so it was that when Utu the sun god rose in the sky, water began to flow in Dilmun. A great river wound its way through the city, a river on which to build a quay, on which to sail boats, and Dilmun was able to trade with other peoples. Water flowed through the canals, watering the fields, and the crops grew in abundance. Ponds filled with good, sweet water, and the beasts drank their fill. Wells filled with good, sweet water, and the people drank their fill.

Then Enki invited the goddess Ninhursag to lie with him. "Come," he said, "let us delight in one another."

Ninhursag lay with Enki, and he poured his seed into her, and she was got with child. For nine days did Ninhursag carry that child, and each day was like a month. After nine days, the child was born, a girl named Ninsar.

One day, Enki went down to the riverbank, and there he saw Ninsar, who was walking along the river on the other side, Ninsar who had grown into a beautiful, young woman. Enki went to his counselor, Isimud, and said, "Is Ninsar not of an age to be kissed? Is she not ready to know a man?"

Isimud answered, "Yes, indeed, she is of an age. Come, get into my boat, and I will sail you over to her."

Enki crossed the river in Isimud's boat. He went to Ninsar and kissed her. Enki took Ninsar and laid her on the ground and poured his seed into her. He poured his seed into her, and she was got with child. For nine days did Ninsar carry that child, and each day was like a month. After nine days, the child was born, a girl named Ninkura.

On another day, Enki went down to the riverbank, and there he saw Ninkura, who was walking along the river on the other side, Ninkura who had grown into a beautiful, young woman. Enki went to his counselor, Isimud, and said, "Is Ninkura not of an age to be kissed? Is she not ready to know a man?"

Isimud answered, "Yes, indeed, she is of an age. Come, get into my boat, and I will sail you over to her."

Enki crossed the river in Isimud's boat. He went to Ninkura and kissed her. Enki took Ninkura and lay her on the ground and poured his seed into her. He poured his seed into her, and she was got with child. For nine days did Ninkura carry that child, and each day was like a month. After nine days, the child was born, a girl named Uttu.

When Uttu came of age, her great-grandmother Ninhursag took her aside and said, "Uttu, you are now of an age where men may begin to look upon you and desire you. You must be very careful when you walk down at the river's edge. Be careful, because Enki often stands on the opposite bank and watches the young women as they go by. If Enki approaches you, do not give him what he wants right away. Tell him that he must first bring to you cucumbers and grapes and apples, all ripe and sweet and juicy, and that when he does so, he will have what he desires."

And so it was that one day Uttu went walking along the riverbank, and she was very beautiful to behold. On the other side of the river, Enki watched Uttu, and he desired her. Once again, Enki's counselor sailed him to the other side of the river, and Enki made known his desire to Uttu.

Uttu remembered Ninhursag's instruction and said, "You will have what you desire only when you bring me cucumbers and grapes and apples, all ripe and sweet and juicy."

"How shall I do that," said Enki, "when all the fields are dry and dusty, and the gardener weeps under his withering trees?"

"I do not know how you are to do those things, only that you will not have what you desire without them."

Enki went to the garden, where all was dry and dusty. He made water flow into the canals. He made water flow into the channels. He made water flow into the furrows. Soon, the garden was bearing all manner of good things, and the gardener danced in his joy. The gardener gave cucumbers, grapes, and apples to Enki, all ripe and sweet and juicy. The gardener heaped cucumbers, grapes, and apples into the lap of Enki, as thanks for the water that made his garden flourish.

Enki took the cucumbers, grapes, and apples to the house of Uttu. He knocked upon her door. From within, Uttu said, "Who is there?"

"It is I, the gardener, bearing cucumbers and grapes and apples," said Enki.

Uttu let him in with great joy. Enki gave to her the cucumbers, grapes, and apples, all ripe and sweet and juicy. And in Uttu's house, they lay together and delighted in one another. Enki poured his seed into Uttu's womb, but Uttu lamented having lain with him. Ninhursag then took the seed from Uttu and planted it in her garden. From Enki's seed grew eight plants with their fruit, and Ninhursag tended them.

One day, Enki said to his counselor Isimud, "Tell me, what of the plants that grew from my seed that Ninhursag planted? Are they grown? Have they fruited? Go to Ninhursag's garden, and see what is growing there."

And so, Isimud went to Ninhursag's garden. He looked over the wall and saw the eight plants growing there, the eight tall plants with their fruit. He saw that the fruit was good to eat and thought that his master might wish to taste of it. So, Isimud cut down the eight plants. He cut them down with their fruit and brought them back to Enki. Enki tasted of their fruit, and it was very good.

When Ninhursag found out that Isimud had cut down the plants and taken them to Enki that he might eat of them, she flew into a rage and cursed Enki. "Never again shall I look upon you!" she said, and then she went away and did not come back.

The Annunaki waited and waited for Ninhursag to return. When she did not, the Annunaki became despondent. They sat in the dust and mourned the loss of Ninhursag.

A fox trotted past and saw the Annunaki and their sorrow. The fox said, "Why is it that you sit in the dust in mourning?"

The Annunaki answered, "We mourn because Ninhursag has left us, and she does not return."

"What will you give me if I return her to you?" said the fox.

Enlil replied, "If you bring back Ninhursag, I will plant a garden for you. I will plant an orchard for you, and your name will always be remembered of the people and the gods."

[The next portion of the story is missing from the tablets. From what little remains, we can gather that the fox disguises himself in some way and is able to get Ninhursag to return to the Annunaki, where she finds them still sitting in the dust in mourning.]

Ninhursag went to Enki where he sat despondent in the dust. Ninhursag said to him, "O my brother, what is it that hurts you?"

Enki said, "My ... it is that hurts me."

Ninhursag said, "I gave birth to the god Abu for you that you might be healed. What else is it that hurts you?"

"My jaw it is that hurts me."

Ninhursag said, "I gave birth to the god Nintul for you that you might be healed. What else is it that hurts you?"

"My tooth it is that hurts me."

Ninhursag said, "I gave birth to the goddess Ninsutu for you that you might be healed. What else is it that hurts you?"

"My mouth it is that hurts me."

Ninhursag said, "I gave birth to the goddess Ninkasi for you that you might be healed. What else is it that hurts you?"

"My ... hurts me."

Ninhursag said, "I gave birth to the goddess Nazi for you that you might be healed. What else is it that hurts you?"

"My arm it is that hurts me."

Ninhursag said, "I gave birth to the goddess Azimua for you that you might be healed. What else is it that hurts you?"

"My side it is that hurts me."

Ninhursag said, "I gave birth to the goddess Ninti for you that you might be healed. What else is it that hurts you?"

"My ... hurts me."

Ninhursag said, "I gave birth to the god Enshagag for you that you might be healed."

Then Ninhursag said, "And now let us say what is to become of these gods and goddesses I have birthed. Abu shall be lord of the plants. Nintul shall be the lord of Magan. Ninsutu shall marry Ninazu, son of Enlil and Ninlil. Ninkasi shall satisfy all desires. Nazi shall marry the god Nindara. Azimua shall marry Ningishzida, son of Ninazu. Ninti shall be queen of the months, and Enshagag shall rule over Dilmun as lord."

The Exploits of Ninurta

The hero-god who slays the monstrous beast is a commonplace figure in world mythology. In the ancient Middle East, this role was played by the god Ninurta. Ninurta is the son of Enlil and Ninhursag and was originally associated with agriculture and fertility. He also is posited as a judge who rules upon points of law.

In this story, Ninurta must fight the Asag, a type of demon or dragon who is going about the land fomenting rebellion against the gods. The Asag recruits stone warriors to help him, and none but Ninurta has the strength to defeat the Asag and his army.

Besides being a tale of heroic deeds and dragon-slaying, this story also explains the origins of irrigation and agriculture as practices initiated by Ninurta in the wake of the Asag's death and assigns the title "Ninhursag," which means something like "Lady of the Wild Hills," to the goddess Ninmah. The myth of Ninurta's exploits also explains the uses and qualities of several different types of stone. While the names of some of the stones have been translated, the identification of most others remains obscure. The section of the myth in which Ninurta declares the fates of the stones is lengthy and somewhat abstruse; here it has been telescoped for a modern audience.

The hero Ninurta sat among the Annunaki at the feast that was called to honor him. Everyone was rejoicing, especially Ninurta, who drank and drank. Even more than An, even more than Enlil did Ninurta drink. And while they were feasting, Bau, goddess of healing, brought before him petitions and Ninurta, son of Enlil, gave his rulings upon them.

As Ninurta decided and the Annunaki feasted, the Sharur, the mighty battle-mace of Ninurta, suddenly cried out, saying, "O my master, O Lord Ninurta, O Ninurta, hero who is the mightiest of all and whom none may withstand, I tell you that the Asag has come forth and is wreaking havoc upon the land. The Asag is a warrior, a fell creature who has no father and who grew and was nourished despite never suckling at the breast. He is arrogant and ambitious, and he comes forth to challenge all.

"The Asag lives in the mountains, and its offspring are many. Even the plants count him king among them. He has called the stones to him. He has called emery and diorite, flint and alabaster, and many more besides, and made an army of them, and with that army, he raids cities far and near. Even the gods of those cities bow before his might, and now, the Asag sits in majesty and metes out justice, usurping the place of the gods. The people live in terror of the Asag, and even the mountains make offerings to him.

"Listen to my words, O mighty one! Listen to what I have to say, for I bring you the pleas of the people. They ask you to come to them and to rid them of the Asag, for none may stand against it but you, O son of Enlil! Be swift in your decision, for day by day your power among the people wanes. They say that if you will not help them, then you will no longer be king over them, and the Asag in his arrogance believes that he can take your place. Day by day he moves into new places and conquers them. Soon, all the Earth will be in his thrall if you do not act!

"But you are the raging bull, you are the swift antelope, and surely you will conquer the Asag. You will conquer the Asag even though his armies are too numerous to be counted, even though no hero has yet been able to defeat the Asag, even though no weapon has yet been able to wound the Asag. What say you, O mighty one? What say you to the insolence of the Asag, to his conquest of cities that rightfully belong to the gods?"

Ninurta heard the words of the Sharur, and he rose out of his seat, crying, "Alas!" He cried with such a great voice that the Earth shook and the heavens trembled. Enlil and the other gods also were shaken and left the E-kur. Mountains fell down before Ninurta's cry, and the Earth was darkened. Ninurta raged in his anger against the Asag, and the Annunaki fled before his anger. Then Ninurta took up his mace and his lance and readied himself for battle. Evil winds he summoned to his aid, winds that brought down a rain of hot coals that consumed all they touched, winds that toppled every tree in their path, winds that made waves upon the Tigris and stirred up her sediments so that her waters were muddied.

Ninurta went to the quay to take a ship on his way to meet the Asag. At the riverside, all the people quailed at the rage of Ninurta. They ran away, blinded by their fear. The birds tried to flee, but the winds of Ninurta made their wings useless. The fish tried to flee, but the storms of Ninurta flung them up onto the shore, where they lay gasping and drowning in air. The cattle and sheep tried to flee, but the fire of Ninurta's anger roasted them where they stood. Even the mountains could not withstand Ninurta's rage, for the floodwaters rose up their banks and washed away everything in their path.

Striding into the lands held by the Asag, Ninurta laid waste their cities; he made captives of their people. He slew the messengers of the Asag; he caused a flood of poison to run through the land, killing all it touched. The rage of Ninurta engulfed the land, and none could withstand his onslaught.

Rejoicing in battle, Ninurta turned to the Sharur and smiled upon it. The Sharur flew away by itself, bringing down mountains for Ninurta, taking prisoners for him, and flying high above the Earth to see what might be seen. Those who saw it flying would give it news to take back to its master, news about the Asag and his armies. When all the news had been gathered, the Sharur returned to Ninurta and said, "Lo! O mighty Ninurta, whose strength none might resist, you have conquered the rebellious places, and already you have slain many of the Asag's warriors. But do not go yet into the mountains to meet the Asag! Verily you are well made and well born, verily you are most beautiful, verily you are greatest in strength and all tremble before you, but do not meet the Asag yet! Do not take your army into the mountains! The time is not yet ripe, and you will not be victorious!"

Ninurta heard the wise words of the Sharur, but he did not heed them. Instead, he marshalled his armies and marched them into the mountains. The Asag saw the approach of Ninurta and armed himself for battle. He pulled down the sky itself and fashioned it into a club. The Asag slithered along the ground like a serpent, ravening like a mad dog. The Asag fell upon Ninurta, howling its rage with a voice that was heard in every corner of the Earth, and none could withstand the passage of that fell beast throughout the land. The waters dried up in their courses, and the trees toppled onto the ground. The reeds were set aflame at the riverside, and the Asag's body carved great furrows into the ground, leaving the Earth gaping with wounds. All the people fled before the Asag as the sky turned red as blood and the crops rotted in the fields. An himself was overwhelmed, Enlil himself fled and hid from the approach of the Asag, and all the Annunaki trembled and sighed with fear.

Enlil cried out, "Who is there to protect us now that Ninurta has gone away to war? Who will keep us safe while the great hero is gone away?"

[The next section is fragmentary, but apparently, the Sharur goes to speak with Enlil about the Asag. Enlil makes a statement encouraging Ninurta to battle fiercely, and the Sharur returns to Ninurta with its report.]

The Sharur returned to its master and said, "O my master, Enlil has spoken, and this is what he says: 'Go forth, O mighty Flood! Go forth and take the Asag. Grip him by the shoulder, impale him on your spear. Take him captive, and drag him here to the E-kur. Do this, and you will never want for praise from all the peoples.'

"Go forth, O my master!" said the Sharur. "Go forth and assail the Asag, for he has built himself a rampart. He has built himself a fortress that cannot be breached, and his lust for destruction never abates."

Ninurta took heart from the words of the Sharur and of Enlil. Ninurta let forth his battle cry, and the day darkened as though it were night.

The Sharur flew into the heavens, raising a great wind that scattered the people like dry leaves. The great mace went to the mountains and set them ablaze. It went through the ranks of the enemy and crushed their skulls. Ninurta's mighty lance flew through the air, and wherever it landed, it opened a crack in the earth. The cracks filled with blood, and the stray dogs licked it up. Ninurta's weapons wrought great destruction throughout the land, and the Asag saw it but was not dismayed.

The Sharur returned to Ninurta and said, "All we do is to no avail! My lord, do not bring battle to the Asag, for he is the foul stench of a festering wound and the pus that flows from it. No matter what you command him to do, he will not obey. Wherever he goes, the land is laid waste and barren, and no one can capture him or withstand his approach. The Asag has dried up all the waters and blows through the lands like a whirlwind. The people cower in their homes, for none may stand against the Asag."

But Ninurta would not stand aside. He faced the mountains and let out a full-throated battle cry, a cry of an entire army calling for death. Ninurta strode about the country, dealing death to all his enemies. The great hero raged about, and from his mountain perch, the Asag saw the fury of the hero Ninurta. Soon enough, Ninurta rampaged his way up the Asag's mountain, and the Asag quailed at the fury of the great hero's approach. The Asag was scattered like drops of water; he was uprooted like weeds from a field. Ninurta flew at the Asag, and in his fury, he crushed the Asag like a grindstone crushes grain in a mill. And not until the foul creature lay dead at Ninurta's feet did the rage of Ninurta begin to subside.

The sun finally set at the end of that terrible day. Ninurta went to the river and washed his weapons in the flowing water. He washed the blood from his clothing and armor, and he washed the blood from his own body. And when all had been cleansed, he stood astride the body of the Asag and sang a victory song.

In the calm that followed the battle, the Annunaki came to where Ninurta stood over the body of the Asag. The gods saw the broken body of that huge monster and marveled at the strength of Ninurta. They prostrated themselves at the feet of the hero and gave him praise for his deeds. The Sharur also praised Ninurta, saying, "None can compare to you, O Ninurta! None can match your strength or your valor! Behold how the gods prostrate themselves at your feet!"

Ninurta addressed the assembled gods. "From this day henceforth, the name of this creature shall not be Asag. Instead, we shall call it Stone, and its entrails shall become the Underworld."

Then Ninurta rested from his labors. He set aside his club, and he rested from his battles.

It was at that time that the land began to dry up. The streams and wells went dry. The Tigris itself shriveled up, and its waters did not reach the sea. Workers went out with shovels and hoes, they went out to dig canals to bring water to the fields, but there was no water to be had. The crops withered in the fields, and the farmers had nothing to bring to market. Famine settled upon the land. No one had the strength to till the fields, and the grain sat scattered upon the soil.

Ninurta looked upon the people in their drought and famine and took pity upon them. He went into the mountains and made a great pile of stones and put into it a sluice gate. He gathered together the waters of the mountains and then let them flow through the sluice into the Tigris. The waters flooded into the riverbed and then up over the banks and into the fields. Soon everywhere there was enough water, and the barley grew heavy with grain in the fields, and the trees in the orchards grew heavy with fruit. The people rejoiced in this. They traded their harvest with peoples of other nations, and they gave great thanks to Ninurta and his father.

Now, at this time, the goddess Ninmah looked upon what her son Ninurta had wrought in the mountains, and she sorrowed because the mountains were no longer a place where she could go. So, Ninmah made a song of lament and went to Ninurta and sang it. Ninmah sang, "I sing 'alas' for the mountains, for they have bowed before the might of Ninurta. I sing 'alas' for the mountains, for they could not withstand his strength, the strength of the mighty hero I bore for the god Enlil. The son of Enlil will not turn his gaze to me, but I shall go to him and gaze upon him. I shall go to him with my lament, and he will see my tears."

Ninurta hearkened to the lament of Ninmah, and he said to her, "Lady Ninmah, well do I remember that when I went into the dangers of battle, you were always there with me. Behold, I have made a pile of stones here, and let this become a new mountain, and you shall be Ninhursag, which is 'Lady of the Mountain.' And I decree that your mountain shall become fecund and a place of great joy. It will bring forth herbs and grasses and fragrant cedars. It will bring forth fruit trees heavy with fruit. In its heart will be gold and silver and all manner of gems. On its sides, the wild beasts and birds will multiply. And you shall have no rival there on that mountain, not even the god An shall approach your queenly splendor. This is my gift to you, O great lady. Rejoice, and be exalted!"

When Ninurta had finished decreeing the fate of the mountains, the lady Aruru, the eldest sister of Enlil, came to him and said, "My lord, you are the greatest hero of them all. You have decreed the fate of the mountains, but what of the fate of those you slew in your battle with the Asag?"

And so, Ninurta addressed the fate of the stone warriors who had sided with the Asag. To the emery stone, flint, and others who had turned against him, Ninurta pronounced punishments. To the alabaster, diorite, hematite, and other stones who had fought on Ninurta's side, he gave great honors.

When all the fates of the stones had been assigned, Ninurta made his way out of the mountains and across the desert. Whenever he came across a village or a city, the people gathered to rejoice over him and sing his praises. On and on he strode, until he came to the river where his own barge was moored, and there the boatmen bowed down before him and sang a song praising him for his deeds. "Who is like Ninurta? Who has his strength or his skill? No enemy can stand against him! Praise to the son of Enlil!"

Then Enlil looked upon Ninurta and gave him a blessing. "O Ninurta, great is your courage and your strength! It was wise to send you to meet the Asag, for none other could have defeated him. All of your enemy's cities have been reduced to ruins, and their rulers made captive. As your reward, you shall receive a heavenly mace and power to rule over all, and eternal life besides."

And so it was that Ninurta killed the Asag, gathered up a pile of stones, and brought the waters down into the fields to make them bear grain and fruit in their seasons. So well had Ninurta healed the land that great mounds of grain were harvested and placed into the granaries. Ninurta gave the grain and the granaries into the care of the lady Nisaba, she who makes green things grow upon the Earth.

The Journey of Nanna to Nippur

One subgenre of Sumerian myth is that of a god's journey to the Sumerian city of Nippur, the primary cult center of the god Enlil, who stood at the head of the Sumerian pantheon. Such journey myths are extant for the gods Enki and Ninurta, in addition to the myth about Nanna presented here. In this story, the moon god Nanna (also known as Nanna-Suen, Suen, or Sin) determines that he should leave his home city of Ur, where his own primary cult center was located, to go to Nippur to visit his mother, the goddess Ninlil, and his father, the god Enlil. Nanna therefore causes a barge to be constructed and lades it with all manner of goods to take home as gifts.

The barge's progress along the river from Ur to Nippur has a ritual aspect in that at every city along the way, the local goddess comes out to greet Nanna and make offerings and grant well wishes, but the barge tells each one that it cannot stop for it is bound for Nippur. Assyriologist Jeremy Black notes that the list of bypassed cities likely reflects actual places one might have expected to encounter along a river journey between Ur and Nippur in ancient times. Further, Black notes that the myth of Nanna's journey reinforces Nanna's function as a god of both fertility and agriculture, especially in his causing an increase in his flocks and herds so that he can give the young produced by his animals as gifts.

There came a time when the god Nanna decided to make a journey to Nippur. Nippur was the city of his father, Enlil, and of his mother, Ninlil. "I shall journey to Nippur," Nanna said, "for I have a mind to visit my mother and my father. I have a mind to visit the lovely city of Nippur and its beautiful sanctuary. I have a mind to visit the strong city of Nippur where the palm trees grow, where palm trees grew even before Dilmun existed. I have a mind to visit the city of my mother who dresses always in the finest linen garments."

It was a long river journey from Nanna's city of Ur to Nippur, and so, Nanna would need a barge, for he wished to take many good gifts to his mother and father. Nanna sent far and wide for the materials to make his barge. Reeds came from Tummal, and pitch from the Apsu. Cypress and cedar, pine and juniper came from the forests and the mountains. When all the needed things were assembled, the workmen began to build the barge.

While the barge was being constructed, Nanna assembled all the gifts he wanted to bring to his parents. Nanna chose fine bulls and sheep from his flocks. He gathered up turtles and birds and fish. Nanna filled many baskets with fresh eggs to take to Enlil's house in Nippur.

Nanna turned loose the rams among his flock of sheep, and six hundred of his ewes dropped fine lambs as gifts for Enlil. Nanna turned male goats loose among his herd of goats, and six hundred female goats dropped fine kids as gifts for Enlil. Nanna did the same with his herds of cattle, letting the bulls loose among the cows, and six hundred cows gave birth to fine calves to be taken as gifts for Enlil.

When the barge was made well and sturdily, and when it was all laden with the gifts of Nanna to Enlil and Ninlil, it set sail along the river. The barge departed Ur and sailed along the river toward Enegir. As the barge approached Enegir, the goddess Ningirida came out of her house and set out an offering of flour. She brought with her a great vat of oil, and she cried out, "Let me anoint you with this fine oil! May you ever have wine and all good things in abundance!"

But the barge did not stop at Enegir. It sailed past, crying out, "I cannot stop! I am bound for Nippur!"

The barge departed Enegir and sailed along the river to Larsa. As the barge approached Larsa, the goddess Sherida came out of her house and set out an offering of flour. She brought with her a great vat of oil, and she cried out, "Let me anoint you with this fine oil! May you ever have wine and all good things in abundance!"

But the barge did not stop at Larsa. It sailed past, crying, "I cannot stop! I am bound for Nippur!"

The barge departed Larsa and sailed along the river to Uruk. As the barge approached Uruk, the goddess Inanna came out of her house and set out an offering of flour. She brought with her a great vat of oil, and she cried out, "Let me anoint you with this fine oil! May you ever have wine and all good things in abundance!"

But the barge did not stop at Uruk. It sailed past, crying, "I cannot stop! I am bound for Nippur!"

The barge departed Uruk and sailed along the river to Shuruppag. As the barge approached Shuruppag, the goddess Ninunuga came out of her house and set out an offering of flour and bran. She brought with her a great vat of oil, and she cried out, "Let me anoint you with this fine oil! May you ever have wine and all good things in abundance!"

But the barge did not stop at Shuruppag. It sailed past, crying, "I cannot stop! I am bound for Nippur!"

The barge departed Shuruppag and sailed along the river to Tummal. As the barge approached Tummal, the goddess Ninlil came out of her house and set out an offering of flour and bran. She brought with her a great vat of oil, and she cried out, "Let me anoint you with this fine oil! May you ever have wine and all good things in abundance!"

But the barge did not stop at Tummal. It sailed past, crying, "I cannot stop! I am bound for Nippur!"

At last, the barge departed Tummal and sailed to Nippur. Nanna sailed the barge to the quay that belonged to Enlil, and there he docked. Nanna called out to the porter who kept the gates of Enlil, "O Kalkal! O porter of my father's house! Open the door to me! Open the gates of my father's house!

"Behold, I, Nanna, have come with a barge laden with many gifts. I have bulls and sheep and goats. I have turtles and small birds. I have fish and I have eggs. Open the door to me!

"I, Nanna, on my journey did bring the lambs that were dropped by the ewes of my flock and the kids that were dropped by the goats of my flock and the calves that were dropped by the cows of my herd. All of these I gave as gifts as I sailed along the Surungal Canal, and my barge is heavy yet with gifts to be given to Enlil and Ninlil. Open the door, Kalkal! Open the door of my father's house!"

Kalkal heard the cry of Nanna, son of Enlil, and in great joy, he opened the gates to him. And there, in the house of Enlil, did Nanna give his gifts to his mighty father, and joyously did Enlil receive them.

"Welcome, my son!" cried Enlil. "Welcome again to my house! Let us eat together! Let us eat of sweet cakes together and of bread and beer!" Enlil called to his servants and commanded them to bring cakes for Nanna to eat. He commanded his servants to gather bread and beer from the E-kur to be given to Nanna to eat.

Nanna ate all the good food Enlil put before him and drank all the good drink, and he said, "O my father, O mighty Enlil, truly I am content with this good food and this good drink. Truly you are the god who gives all in abundance!

"Now it is time for me to return home to Ur, but first I ask you to fill my rivers with good fish. I ask you to fill my fields with barley heavy in the ear. Give me reeds along the rivers and wild sheep in the hills. Give me good trees in the forest and fruit for syrup and wine in the orchards. And give to me a long life, for it is time for me to return home to Ur!"

Everything Nanna asked for, Enlil gave him. He filled the rivers with good fish and the fields with barley heavy in the ear. Enlil gave Nanna reeds along the rivers and wild sheep in the hills. Enlil gave Nanna good trees in the forest and fruit for syrup and wine in the orchards, and to Nanna himself, he gave a long life.

Praise be to Enlil where he sits on his throne, and to Ninlil, mother of Nanna!

Inanna and Ebih

Male deities such as Ninurta are not the only ones who go forth to do battle with monstrous creatures in the mountains. In this story, the goddess Inanna girds herself for war to get revenge on Ebih, a mountain that refuses to bow down before her in worship. We see here the more violent of the two sides of Inanna, who in addition to being the goddess of love and procreation was the goddess of war, which is often referred to as "the game of Inanna" in Sumerian texts.

Inanna was one of the more powerful goddesses of the Sumerian pantheon, bearing the title "Queen of Heaven." She later became identified with the Akkadian/Babylonian goddess Ishtar. One myth that explains the origin of Inanna's might says that she stole some of Enki's me, *a Sumerian word denoting power or authority, after Enki had too much to drink at a banquet. Inanna sails with the* me *back to her city of Uruk, fending off the attempts of Enki and his demons to retrieve the stolen powers.*

The myth of Inanna and Ebih retold below, which shows Inanna wielding her powers of vengeance and destruction, names several places that Inanna visits in her wanderings, specifically Elam, Subir, and the Lulubi Mountains. Elam was a region on the northeastern shore of the Persian Gulf, in what is now Iran, while Subir was far to the north of Sumer, in Upper Mesopotamia. The Lulubi Mountains are an area within the Zagros range, in a portion that now lies on the border between Iraq and Iran. In her retelling of this myth, author Betty De Shong Meador notes that Mount Ebih "has been identified as the modern Jebel Hamrin," a mountain ridge that runs along the western side of the Zagros Mountains.

This myth also has special importance as part of the first piece of written literature for which we have the author's name, since it forms part of a longer work called "The Exaltation of Inanna" by a woman named Enheduanna. Enheduanna was the daughter of Sargon of Akkad, founder of the Akkadian Empire, and was high priestess of both Inanna and Nanna in the Sumerian city of Ur in the 23rd century BCE. "The Exaltation of Inanna" functions both as praise of the goddess and as a semi-autobiographical work, since it references Enheduanna's expulsion from Ur by her brother, Rimush, and her reinstatement in the temple there.

Great was the goddess Inanna, daughter of Nanna the god of the moon, and great her power. Fearsome in battle was she, clad in armor, laying waste to armies with her weapons and the strength of her arm. For her strength was that of the wild bull, and her fierceness in battle that of the lion, her glory was that of the sun shining down upon the Earth, and all the people bowed down before her in fear and praise.

One day, Inanna went forth into the mountains. She went to Elam and Subir. She went into the Lulubi Mountains. She went into the Lulubi Mountains, and there, in the midst of them, was the greatest peak, which was called Ebih. As Inanna passed, all the mountains bowed low before her and did her honor, but Ebih would not bend. Ebih did not bow down to the ground before her; Ebih did not kiss the dust at her feet. This greatly angered Inanna, and she swore she would have vengeance on Ebih for its disrespect.

"Truly shall I make Ebih know my wrath! Truly shall I make it know how it has wronged me! Ebih did not bow down before me, and Ebih did not kiss the dust at my feet. I shall bring battle to the mountains. I shall bring my battering ram and my bow and quiver of arrows. I shall bring my lance and my shield. Fire will I bring to the forests of the mountains and an axe to the boles of its trees. All the mountains shall quail before my rage, and never more shall Ebih hold its head up with pride."

And so, Inanna, daughter of Nanna, put on her garments of battle and her radiant crown whose brilliance was terror to all who beheld it. She took up her seven-headed weapon and put on her sandals of lapis lazuli. When the sun had set, she went to the Gate of Wonder dressed in all her battle array. There she made an offering to An and prayed to him.

An saw Inanna and saw that she was arrayed for battle. He heard her prayer, and he smiled upon her. An sat on his divine throne, and then Inanna came forth to speak to him. "O my father, greetings! You have given me many gifts, and so it is that none can rival me in heaven or on Earth. I am terrible to behold, and none may best me in battle! I am sword and arrow, lance and shield! Kings call upon me, and I answer, and with my aid, they slay their enemies, and thus I bring glory to the name of An.

"Today I went forth into the mountains, and the mountain Ebih did me no honor. The mountain Ebih did not fear me. It did not bow down before me and kiss the dust at my feet. And so it is that I come before you, O Father An, to say that I shall go into the mountains and bring battle to them. I shall use my battering ram and my bow and arrows. I shall use my lance and my shield. Fire will I bring to the mountains and an axe to the boles of its trees. All the mountains shall quail before my rage, and never more shall Ebih hold its head up with pride.

"Let me go forth in battle array. Let me lay low the mountain that refused me the honor I am due. Let me vanquish it, and teach it to respect the goddess Inanna."

An heard the words of Inanna and said, "So you wish to destroy this mountain. Very well, but do you know what task lies before you? What do you really know of this mountain? Let me tell you what task lies before you, this task against a mountain that even the Annunaki have cause to fear. The forests of this mountain are thick, and its orchards heavy with fruit. Under the trees dwell lions, on its flanks dwell wild rams, and stags run through its meadows, where herds of wild bulls graze. This mountain is most fearsome, and you will not be able to vanquish it."

The lady Inanna did not heed the words of An. She strode away from him and pushed open the great gate of the House of the Gods. She strode through the gate in her battle array, her weapons in her hands, and her wrath was terrible to behold. Her wrath was like a great flood, and she called up a whirlwind to rage alongside her.

Inanna went into the mountains, and she brought battle to Ebih. The mountain fought fiercely, but Inanna gave no quarter. She grabbed the neck of Ebih and roared like a lion as she stabbed its vitals with her dagger.

The body of Ebih split and crumbled. The stones of Ebih's body cracked and rolled down its flanks. The serpents who lived in its caves and crevasses spat out venom.

Inanna cursed the forests of the mountain and brought a great drought upon them. She set the forests alight, and the smoke of their burning blotted out the sun. And so it was that Inanna showed that she alone had the power and that she alone was due honor and praise.

Then Inanna spoke to the mountain she had conquered, saying, "O Ebih Mountain, you thought yourself divine because of your height. You thought yourself divine because of your beauty. You thought yourself divine because your peak brushed the very heavens, but you did not know your place. You did not bow down before me and kiss the dust at my feet. And so it is that I have vanquished you and taken all your beauty and might.

"I have vanquished you as I would have done a wild bull. I have conquered you as I would have done an elephant. Behold, now your eyes can do nothing but weep, and your heart can do nothing but mourn, and the birds that nest in what is left of you shall sing songs only of grief.

"I brought to you the terror that was the gift of Enlil to me. I brought you battle with the weapons that were the gifts of Enlil, and with my strength and my weapons, I have brought the mountain down. A palace have I built for myself, and I have given ritual objects to those who carry out the cults of the gods.

"It is I who conquered the mountain. Like a flood, I washed it away. Like a raging wind, I blew it down. I am the victor over Ebih."

Praise be to Inanna, daughter of Nanna!

Praise be to Nisaba!

Dumuzi and Enkimdu

In this myth, the sun god Utu wishes his sister, the goddess Inanna, to marry the god of shepherds, Dumuzi. Inanna herself prefers Enkimdu, the god of farmers. (Enkimdu the farmer is a character distinct from Gilgamesh's friend Enkidu.) Dumuzi is insulted by Inanna's preference; he wants to be Inanna's husband. What follows is a kind of contest between Dumuzi and Enkimdu for the hand of Inanna, in which each god states what they might bring to the marriage.

Many scholars have noted the parallels between the myth of Dumuzi and Enkimdu and the biblical story of Cain and Abel, since both stories involve a quarrel between a shepherd on the one hand and a farmer on the other, encapsulating age-old conflicts between pastoral and agricultural peoples. Unlike the biblical story, however, the Sumerian myth of Dumuzi and Enkimdu ends with the two gods becoming friends and agreeing to exchange the products of their labors with one another. Inanna eventually agrees to marry Dumuzi, but that is not shown in this story.

There was a time when the sun god Utu went to his sister Inanna and said, "O my sister, it is time that you were married. It is time that you chose a husband. I think that you should marry the god of shepherds, Dumuzi. He has many fine sheep, and his ewes drop healthy lambs in their season. The milk of his goats is the best in the land, and the butter and cheese of his sheep cannot be rivaled. He would be the best husband for you."

"I'll not wed a shepherd!" cried Inanna. "I'll not wed a shepherd and wear garments of wool. I'll not wed a shepherd, no! A farmer shall be my husband. A farmer who grows grain that waves in the wind and bows down low when it is heavy in the ear. A farmer who grows good flax for fine linen. Him will I wed!"

Dumuzi heard the words of Inanna, and he said to her, "Why? Why do you prefer the farmer over me? What does the farmer Enkimdu have that I lack? He might have a good black robe, but he can trade that to me for a black ewe. He might have a good white robe, but he can trade that to me for a white ewe. He might brew good beer, but he can trade that to me for some of my goats' milk. Bread he can give to me in exchange for milk, and lentils he can give me in exchange for cheese. He can come and dine with me, and I will even give him extra butter and extra milk!"

Then Dumuzi took his sheep down to the riverbank to graze, and he was happy there with his flock. While Dumuzi watched over his sheep, Enkimdu came to him and said, "Why do you compare yourself to me, O shepherd? What reason have we to quarrel? Your sheep graze happily here by the river; I will also let them graze on the stubble after my crops have been harvested. Your sheep drink water happily from the river; I will also let them drink from the canal that waters my land."

Dumuzi listened to the words of Enkimdu, and then he said, "O farmer, let me count you as my friend. I think we should be friends, you and I."

"That is well," said Enkimdu, "and I shall share with you my barley and lentils. And also I shall bring barley and lentils to the lady Inanna, or whatever else shall be her pleasure."

The Marriage of Martu

Martu is the Sumerian name for the Akkadian god Amurru. The name "Amurru" also refers to a nomadic people who lived in the hills rather than in the more urbanized river valleys. Modern readers may know the Amurru people as "Amorites," a Semitic-speaking nomadic tribe mentioned in the Old Testament who originated in what is now modern Syria. The Amorites did not always live in peace with Sumerian and Akkadian peoples; from time to time, the Amorites would conduct raids on settlements in the Mesopotamian lowlands. City-dwelling Sumerians and Akkadians thought of the Amorites as barbarians, but it was the Amorites who flooded into and eventually took over large parts of southern Mesopotamia starting in the 22nd century BCE and who eventually founded the first great dynasty of the city of Babylon, which became one of the most important urban centers in the ancient world.

In the myth retold below, the god Martu is a member of a nomadic tribe who find themselves in the vicinity of a city called Inab, where a festival to honor the god Numushda is about to be held. Martu wishes to marry, and when he wins a wrestling competition held in honor of Numushda, he declares that his prize will be none other than the god's own daughter, Adgarkidu. One of Adgarkidu's friends is horrified over the match, since in her eyes Martu is an unwashed, unlettered barbarian not worthy to wed the city-dwelling Adgarkidu, but Adgarkidu declares, "I shall marry Martu!" This story, therefore, represents the merging of two cultures, that of the nomadic hill-dwelling Amorites and that of the agricultural and urban settlements of the Tigris and Euphrates Valleys.

Once there was a fine city called Inab. It was well built and well appointed, and its people were prosperous. In the lands around Inab lived tribes of nomads. These nomads lived by capturing gazelles with nets, and every evening, the men would go to the center of their camp to receive their rations. By the law of their god, unmarried men received a single ration. Men with a wife but no children received double, and men with a wife and a child received triple.

Among these people was a man named Martu, who was brave, handsome, and strong. He went to receive his ration, but every time, he received a double portion, even though he was unmarried. This troubled Martu, for it meant that he was receiving more than his friends, even those who were married, since they had to share their double portion with their wives.

Martu went to his mother and said, "It is not right that I should receive a double portion even though I am unmarried. It is not right that I should receive more than my married friends do. I have a mind to take a wife. What should I do?"

Martu's mother said, "If you wish to marry, choose the woman carefully. Choose a woman you can love and cherish. Take a woman you can choose for yourself."

Martu decided to follow his mother's advice. He started looking for a woman to marry, but he found none among his own people. But soon there was to be a great festival in the city of Inab, a festival in honor of the god Numushda. Martu rejoiced at this, for he could both participate in the festival and look for a wife. "Come," Martu said to his companions, "let us go to the festival together. We will enjoy ourselves and honor the god, and perhaps I shall find a wife."

And so, Martu and his friends went to Inab for the festival. There they saw the god Numushda, who was there with his wife, Namrat, and his daughter, Adgarkidu. The celebrations were very joyous. Musicians played loudly upon drums all throughout the city, and in the temple of Numushda, the young men gathered to compete in wrestling competitions in his honor.

Martu went to the temple and entered the competition for he loved to wrestle, and he desired to honor the god as was right and proper to do. In every bout, Martu was the victor. No one could match him for strength or skill. Every one of the men who wrestled against him was defeated. Many went home wounded, and a few died, for they could not withstand Martu's great strength.

Numushda watched the wrestling competition, and he marveled at the strength and skill of Martu. When he saw that Martu had defeated all the other wrestlers, Numushda rejoiced greatly. He went to Martu and said, "Lo, you have brought me great honor this day! Let me reward you as you deserve. I shall give you much silver as your reward."

Martu bowed to the god and said, "The lord Numushda is most generous, but I do not desire silver."

"What, then?" said Numushda. "Will you accept gold? Jewels? I am rich beyond compare, and I will share my wealth with you."

"Neither gold nor jewels are my desire. I wish to marry your daughter, Adgarkidu, for I have seen her there with you, watching the competition, and my heart is given to her."

"Very well," said Numushda, "but if you are to marry her, you must pay a bride price worthy of the daughter of a god."

"Name your price, and I shall pay it," said Martu.

"My price is calves. Many calves, with their mothers to give milk, and a bull to breed with."

"That price I can pay," said Martu.

"My price also is lambs. Many lambs, with their mothers to give milk, and a fine ram to breed with."

"That price I can pay," said Martu.

"My price also is kids. Many kids, with their mothers to give milk, and a fine he-goat to breed with."

"All of your price I can pay," said Martu, "and more besides."

Martu paid the price to Numushda as he promised, and he gave many fine gifts of gold and silver to the people of Inab. Also he gave them fine garments to wear, of many colors, and shawls for the old women.

The days went by, but still the marriage feast had not been held. Adgarkidu's friend watched the preparations and saw how Martu paid his bride price, but she thought very little of Martu, despite his generosity, his strength, and his good looks. The friend went to Adgarkidu and said, "Why are you marrying that Martu? He really is not worthy of you. Don't you know that he and his people live out in the open, in tents, with only the hide of goats to keep out the wind and the rain? They roam everywhere in the wilderness, like animals. I'll wager Martu doesn't even know how to honor the gods properly. He probably knows none of the prayers and none of the rituals. I've even heard that people like him eat their meat raw! Surely you cannot think to marry Martu!"

But Adgarkidu simply looked at her friend and said, "I shall marry Martu!"

Part II: Tales of Kings and Heroes

Enmerkar and the Ensuhkeshdanna

Enmerkar was the legendary first king of Uruk, who was deified and the subject of several myths. Enmerkar is credited with having built the city of Uruk, one of the principal ancient Sumerian cities situated between the Tigris and Euphrates Rivers in what is now southern Iraq. Enmerkar also is described as the father of Lugalbanda, the legendary second king of Uruk and the grandfather of Gilgamesh, an actual historical personage whose exploits became mythologized in the ancient Epic of Gilgamesh.

Tales about Enmerkar often state that he is the son of Utu, the sun god, which also makes him a nephew to the goddess Inanna, the tutelary goddess of Uruk. In the story retold below, Enmerkar is engaged in a rivalry with Ensuhkeshdanna, the lord of Aratta, a mythical city that is described in various tales as beautiful and supremely wealthy. Here Enmerkar and Ensuhkeshdanna are fighting over which one of them is more entitled to the favors of

Inanna. The two kings undertake their fight for supremacy by means of contests between their chief sorcerers.

Once there were two cities, Uruk and Aratta. Enmerkar, son of Utu, was lord over Uruk, and Ensuhkeshdanna was lord over Aratta. One day, Ensuhkeshdanna had a mind to begin a rivalry with Enmerkar, and so he summoned his messenger and said to him, "Go you to the city of Uruk, and take this message to Enmerkar. Tell Enmerkar that he should submit to me because although he might enjoy the favors of Inanna on a beautiful bed, I enjoy her on an even more splendid bed. And although Enmerkar might see her while she sleeps at night, I see her during the day and hold converse with her. Enmerkar might have a fine flock of geese, but mine is even better, and if Enmerkar does not submit, he will have to beg me to have geese from my flock."

The messenger ran to Uruk with the swiftness of a hawk in flight and went before Enmerkar to deliver his message. "My Lord Enmerkar, Ensuhkeshdanna, lord of Aratta, begs me to tell you this: 'Enmerkar should submit to me because although he might enjoy the favors of Inanna on a beautiful bed, I enjoy her on an even more splendid bed. And although Enmerkar might see her while she sleeps at night, I see her during the day and hold converse with her. Enmerkar might have a fine flock of geese, but mine is even better, and if Enmerkar does not submit, he will have to beg me to have geese from my flock.'"

Enmerkar heard the words of the messenger from Aratta, and he said, "Take this message back to your master. Tell him that while he might lie with Inanna on his own beautiful bed, I lie with her on her own bed that is carved with figures of lions. Enlil himself made me king. When I was a baby, the mighty Ninurta dandled me on his lap, and I nursed at the breast of Aruru, sister to Enlil. Inanna might pay visits to Aratta, but it is in Uruk that she makes her home. And what of your flocks of geese? You have none. Any geese you have will be gotten from me, Enmerkar, King of Uruk."

The messenger ran swiftly back to Aratta and delivered Enmerkar's message to Ensuhkeshdanna. When Ensuhkeshdanna heard Enmerkar's words, he was downcast. "What reply ought I to make to Enmerkar? I tested him, and he bested me for sure."

Ensuhkeshdanna's counselors said, "It was you who first sent a boastful message to Uruk. You need not worry about what he will do; you need to control yourself. Stop vying with Enmerkar; you will achieve nothing good by doing that."

Ensuhkeshdanna scoffed at the advice of his counselors. "Enmerkar might raze my city to the ground, and yet I will be one piece of brick amongst the rubble. I will never submit to the King of Uruk."

Word of the contest between Ensuhkeshdanna and Enmerkar came to the ears of a sorcerer named Urgirinuna, a man from Hamazu. He had come to live in Aratta after his own city was destroyed. Urgirinuna went to Ensuhkeshdanna's vizier and said, "I have heard what passed between Ensuhkeshdanna and Enmerkar. Tell your lord Ensuhkeshdanna that I am a sorcerer and that I can make Uruk submit to Aratta. I can make Uruk and all of its territories bow before the might of Aratta. Enmerkar and the people of Uruk will come here, and instead of living in their own city, they will have to work for us."

The vizier told Ensuhkeshdanna what the sorcerer had said. "This is excellent!" said Ensuhkeshdanna. "Bring the sorcerer to me, that I may give him gold and silver for his journey, and tell him that if he succeeds, he shall have nothing but the choicest food to eat and nothing but the finest wine to drink for the rest of his days."

The sorcerer accepted the money from Ensuhkeshdanna and set out toward the city of Uruk. When he arrived at Uruk, city of the goddess Nisaba, he went into the cow byre. The cow trembled when she saw the sorcerer. "Who drinks your milk and eats your butter?" said the sorcerer, who had the power to speak to animals.

"Nisaba it is who drinks my milk and eats my butter. My cheese graces Nisaba's table," said the cow.

"May your milk go into your horns," said the sorcerer. "May your milk go into your back."

Next the sorcerer went to the pen where the goat was kept. The goat trembled when she saw the sorcerer.

"Who drinks your milk and eats your butter?" said the sorcerer to the goat.

"Nisaba it is who drinks my milk and eats my butter. My cheese graces Nisaba's table," said the goat.

"May your milk go into your horns," said the sorcerer. "May your milk go into your back."

When the cowherd went to milk the cow, he found that she had no milk in her udder, and her calf was crying loudly in hunger. When the goatherd went to milk the goat, he found that she had no milk either, and her kid was crying also. The cowherd and the goatherd wept in despair. They fell down on the ground and prayed to Utu. "O mighty Utu," they said, "the sorcerer from Aratta came here and made the cow and the goat stop giving milk. The animals have no milk to feed their young, and we have no milk to give to the people. Utu, grant us your aid!"

At that time, there was a wise woman named Sagburu who lived in Uruk. She heard what the sorcerer had done to the cow and the goat. "This cannot stand," she said to herself. "I must do something about that evil sorcerer."

And so Sagburu went to speak to Enmerkar. "I know who it is who has made the milk dry up," Sagburu said to the king, "and I shall make him pay for his crime."

"What will you do?" said Enmerkar.

"I shall have a contest of magic with him," she said. "I shall defeat him, and then he will pay the price for his misdeeds."

"Very well," said Enmerkar. "Your reward will be very great if you are successful. Go and challenge the sorcerer with my blessing!"

Soon enough, Sagburu found the sorcerer, who was sitting in the shade of a tree near the river. "Sorcerer!" she said. "I have heard what you did to the cow and the goat of Nisaba. Surely you shall pay for your misdeeds."

The sorcerer stood and faced Sagburu and said, "I will do no such thing. I am the mightiest sorcerer in the land, and I answer to no one, save that they can defeat me in a contest of magic."

"What if I were to accept that challenge?" said Sagburu.

"You? Accept my challenge? I think you will lose," said the sorcerer. "But if you choose defeat, that is your business. So, this is what I propose: we should each throw fish spawn into the river and make animals arise from it. If my animals defeat yours, then I win. If your animals defeat mine, then you win."

"I accept your challenge," said Sagburu.

The woman and the sorcerer each took a handful of fish spawn and threw it into the river. The sorcerer's fish spawn changed into a giant carp that leapt out of the water. The woman's fish spawn turned into an eagle that swooped down upon the carp and caught it in its talons. Then the eagle flew away into the mountains with the carp.

Again, the woman and the sorcerer threw fish spawn into the river. The sorcerer made his fish spawn turn into an ewe and its lamb. The woman made her fish spawn turn into a wolf. The wolf leapt upon the ewe and its lamb and dragged them away into the desert.

A third time they threw fish spawn into the river. The sorcerer made his fish spawn turn into a cow and its calf. The woman made her fish spawn turn into a lion. The lion leapt upon the cow and its calf and dragged them away into the reed beds.

A fourth time they threw fish spawn into the river. The sorcerer made his fish spawn turn into an ibex and a wild sheep. The woman made her fish spawn turn into a leopard. The leopard leapt upon the ibex and the wild sheep and dragged them away into the mountains.

A fifth time they threw fish spawn into the river. The sorcerer made his fish spawn turn into a gazelle kid. The woman made her fish spawn turn into a tiger and a lion. The tiger and the lion leapt upon the gazelle kid and dragged it away into the forest.

The sorcerer saw how the wise woman had defeated him every time, and he quailed. Sagburu said to him, "Sorcerer, you do have some power, but what did you think you would achieve by challenging a wise woman of Uruk? What did you think you would achieve by challenging a wise woman of the city of Nisaba, the city beloved of Ninlil, whose destiny is decreed by none other than Enlil and An?"

"Have mercy on me," said the sorcerer. "I knew nothing of this when I came to Uruk. You have won our contest; I grant that you are the more powerful magician. Please do not harm me. Let me return home to Aratta, and there I will sing your praises to all who will listen."

Sagburu replied, "You came to Uruk, and you frightened the animals. You dried up the udders of the cow and the goat, so that now we have no milk and no butter. You took away the milk, and now we have no cheese to grace our tables. There is no pardon for this offense in Uruk; the law commands it so." Then Sagburu threw the sorcerer into the river and killed him. When Sagburu was sure the sorcerer was dead, she returned home to her city.

When Ensuhkeshdanna found out what had happened to his sorcerer, he sent a messenger to Enmerkar. The messenger came before Enmerkar and said, "Ensuhkeshdanna, my master, bids me tell you this: 'Surely Enmerkar is the favored of Inanna, and you are the first in all the lands. I am not your equal and will never match you.'"

Lugalbanda in the Mountain Cave

This tale is part of a longer narrative detailing deeds of Enmerkar's heroic son, Lugalbanda, who in turn was the father of the great Gilgamesh. The pretext for this story is Enmerkar's desire to wage war on Aratta. During the march of Uruk's army through the Zabu (Zagros) Mountains on their way to Aratta, Lugalbanda is paralyzed by illness, and his friends make the heart-wrenching decision to leave him behind in the hopes that he will recover and rejoin them.

Lugalbanda's companions leave him well provisioned with many kinds of food and drink, as well as his axe and dagger. The translators of this story from the Electronic Text Corpus of Sumerian Literature note that while Lugalbanda's friends hope he will get well again, they are in fact hedging their bets and also preparing him for burial, since the kinds of items they leave with him were part of Sumerian burial traditions. The story also shows the importance of the sun, the moon, and the planet Venus within Sumerian religion, since Lugalbanda prays to each of them for healing once he recovers enough to be able to pray at all. A further point of the story is to show how important and favored Lugalbanda is, since in addition to the three deities who heal him, he is visited by Zangara, the god of dreams, and by four major deities (An, Enlil, Enki, and Ninhursag), who come to eat the offering feast he prepares for them.

There came a time when Enmerkar, King of Uruk, decided to mount a campaign against the city of Aratta. Aratta would not submit to Uruk, and so Enmerkar marshaled his army and prepared for an assault against that strong and beautiful city. The number of men in Enmerkar's army was so great that it was like a flood in numbers and in strength.

When all was ready, Enmerkar led his army on the road to Aratta. Enmerkar marched at the head of his army, and his armor and weapons glinted in the sun. So brightly did they shine that all who saw him did not wonder in the least that this was the very son of Utu. The army of Uruk marched over hills and across plains. For five days, they marched toward Aratta. On the sixth day, they stopped to rest, and on the seventh, they began to march into the mountains.

Now, the captains of Enmerkar's army were seven warriors, champions and heroes all, sons of Urash, the earth goddess, and raised in the very house of An himself. The eighth captain was Enmerkar's son, Lugalbanda, a man both strong and crafty. But while the army was marching through the mountains, Lugalbanda fell gravely ill. He fell to the ground and could neither move nor speak, although he still breathed and his heart still beat. Enmerkar's and Lugalbanda's friends all tried to help him, but nothing they did made any difference.

"We should bring him back to Uruk," said one soldier.

"We cannot," said Enmerkar, "for it is too far to go, and we can spare no one."

"Let us bring him back to Kulaba then," said another.

"We cannot," said Enmerkar, "for it is too far to go, and we can spare no one."

Lugalbanda's friends looked about the place where they had stopped, and they spied a small cave in the side of the mountain. "Let us leave him there," said one, "let us leave him there with provisions and coverings, and maybe the gods will smile upon him and heal him, and he will rejoin us when he is well."

Enmerkar agreed that this was a good plan. The soldiers placed Lugalbanda inside the cave and wrapped him well to keep him warm. They left him a good number of provisions, dates and figs and cheese, bread and butter, wine and beer, all packed into leather bags. Then they prepared some incense in a dish and suspended it from the roof of the cave above Lugalbanda's head. Then they placed his good tin axe and good iron dagger next to him, and during all these preparations, Lugalbanda's eyes were open. He watched what his friends did, and tears flowed down his cheeks, but he was still unable to move or speak.

Lugalbanda's friends said to him, "If you should get well, there is food and drink here to make you strong again. May Utu make you well and bring you home safe to your city of Kulaba. But if Utu should call you to the afterlife, we shall stop here when our business in Aratta is done, and we will bring your body home for proper burial."

Then Enmerkar's and Lugalbanda's friends left the cave, and the army marched on without him, shedding bitter tears all the while, for they all were sure that they would never see the mighty Lugalbanda alive again.

For two days did Lugalbanda lie in that cave, unable either to move or to speak. On the afternoon of the third day, he was able to move a little and speak a little, but he was still very weak and very ill. Lugalbanda raised his hands to the heavens and with many bitter tears prayed to Utu. "O Utu, O shining one, you are ever blessed! I beg you, let me be well again. Let me be well so that I can leave this cave and rejoin my friends. I do not wish to die here, alone and untended by any who care for me. I do not wish for my companions to return here only to find my dead body. O Utu, O shining one, let me be well again!"

Utu heard the prayers of Lugalbanda and spoke to him with words of encouragement, but still Lugalbanda was weak and ill.

When Utu had gone to his rest, Lugalbanda looked out into the sky, and there he saw the brightness of Inanna. Lugalbanda raised his hands to her, and with many bitter tears, he prayed. "O Inanna, O shining one! Here I am in this cave, when I should be with my friends. Here I am, alone and friendless, when I should be in my own beautiful city. Let me be well again! I pray you, O shining one, do not let me die here, alone and friendless!"

Inanna heard the prayers of Lugalbanda. She came into his cave and gave him the gift of healing sleep and the gift of peace in his heart, and then she returned to her own city.

Lugalbanda slept for a time, and when he woke, it was deep night. Lugalbanda looked out into the sky, and there he saw Nanna shining brightly. Lugalbanda lifted his hands to Nanna and with many tears prayed to him. "O bright Nanna, O shining one! Truly you love justice and despise evil! You are mighty in justice and wrathful against those who do evil! Let me be well again, O bright Nanna!"

Nanna heard Lugalbanda's prayers and saw his tears, and he gave to him the movement of his limbs. Once again, Lugalbanda was able to stand.

In the morning, Lugalbanda saw the brightness of Utu as he rose above the horizon. The light of the sun god poured into Lugalbanda's cave, and the evil god who had struck Lugalbanda down departed from him. When Lugalbanda realized he was well again, he said a prayer of thanks to Utu, praising him greatly.

Lugalbanda walked out of the cave, and there he saw healing plants growing and a stream flowing with life-giving water, the gifts of the gods to him. Lugalbanda ate of the plants and drank of the water, and all his strength returned. Rejoicing that he felt well again, Lugalbanda ran through the mountains, swift and surefooted. Then he returned to his cave and packed his weapons and the provisions his companions had left for him, and he set off to find Enmerkar and his army.

After walking for some time, Lugalbanda decided to stop and make camp. He made a fire and baked good bread in the embers. He ate the bread with date syrup. While Lugalbanda was eating, he heard the sound of a great beast tearing at the grass. He looked about him, and there he saw a huge wild bull, eating the grass and drinking from a nearby stream. Lugalbanda lay in ambush for the bull. He seized it by the horns and subdued it, then he tethered it in a place near his camp. Next a herd of goats passed near to Lugalbanda's camp. Lugalbanda went out and captured two fine goats. He seized them, subdued them, then tethered them in a place near his camp.

His meal eaten, the bull and the goats captured, Lugalbanda felt overcome with weariness. He made himself a bed of fresh mountain herbs. Then he took a drink of the good beer his friends had given him, and he lay down to sleep.

While Lugalbanda slept, he had a dream. Zangara, the very god of dreams himself, appeared to Lugalbanda in the guise of a great bull. Zangara bellowed to Lugalbanda, saying, "Who will sacrifice the wild bull for me? Who will sacrifice the wild goats for me? Who will pour out their blood in sacrifice? The one who must do this is he who wields the axe of tin. The one who must do this is he who wields the dagger of iron. Let him make an offering to the gods. Let him offer the bull and the goats to the gods at the break of day."

Lugalbanda awoke from his dream, shivering. He sat for a time in awe at the god's apparition to him. Then he took up his axe and his dagger and did as Zangara commanded. He sacrificed the bull and the goats at the break of day, pouring out their blood into a pit. Lugalbanda prepared the offerings in a banquet for the gods, and lo! Enlil, An, Enki, and Ninhursag came to dine upon the freshly roasted meat. Lugalbanda fed them well on the roasted meat and on the beer and wine he had on hand, and for a libation he poured out fresh water.

Then Lugalbanda set up altars to Nanna and Utu, and he decorated them well with lapis lazuli. For Nanna and Utu, Lugalbanda set out fresh cakes.

[What remains of the story is fragmentary, and the end of the story is lost. The parts that remain depart from a narrative about Lugalbanda and launch into what the Electronic Corpus of Sumerian Literature says is a description of demons. These descriptions pair the demons (or whoever else is being described) with various attributes that are connected to the relevant god or goddess. For example, one line calls them "gazelles of Suen," while another calls them "fine smooth cloths of Ninlil."]

Lugalbanda and the Anzu Bird

This story of the heroic exploits of Lugalbanda continues the narrative of the rivalry between Uruk and the mythical city of Aratta. It also continues the epic of Lugalbanda, explaining how he rejoins the rest of Enmerkar's army after he recovers from the illness that caused his companions to leave him behind in a cave in the Zabu (Zagros) Mountains in the hope that he might recover.

The Zagros is a range that runs from west to east along the southern edge of Turkey, turns southeastward to run along the border between Iraq and Iran, and then farther south along the eastern shore of the Persian Gulf. The Zagros range was both distant from Sumerian lands and home to peoples who occasionally were hostile to the Sumerians; thus, in Sumerian myths, these mountains are painted as a dangerous place that one might enter but not leave alive, as well as a home to strange and fantastic creatures.

One such creature that Lugalbanda encounters in his wanderings is the Anzu Bird. The Anzu Bird or, more simply, "Anzu," is a formidable creature that appears in many Sumerian and Mesopotamian tales, having aspects that are either good or evil depending on when the particular story about the bird was created. The story retold here leans toward presenting the Anzu Bird as vain and fearsome but basically good. Some representations of Anzu in ancient art show him as a lion-headed eagle and others as half-man, half-bird. The Anzu Bird was associated with thunder and storms in ancient Sumerian myths, and although considered a powerful being, it seems to have not enjoyed its own worship cult.

There came a time when Lugalbanda was on campaign with the armies of the cities of Uruk, going out to fight the city of Aratta alongside King Enmerkar, son of Utu, the sun god, and Lugalbanda became separated from his companions. Lugalbanda was lost in the Zabu Mountains and had no one to turn to for advice. As Lugalbanda walked along a mountain path, he spied the nest of the Anzu Bird, a monstrous creature with enormous talons and a serrated beak like the mouth of a shark. The nest was in a great tree, the crown of which spread out even over the highest mountain peaks, and its roots were buried in the mouth of a great river belonging to Utu, god of the sun.

"I know what I shall do," said Lugalbanda. "I shall go to the bird and speak to him graciously. I shall provide good beer and sweet cakes for him and his family. Maybe if I treat him well, he will tell me where my brothers in arms have gone, where I might find the troops of my city Uruk."

Lugalbanda made cakes, sweetening them with golden honey. He went to the Anzu Bird's nest and found inside it a young chick. Lugalbanda fed the sweet cakes to the chick, and also some meat and good sheep's fat. Then he beautified the chick, painting its eyes with kohl and perfuming it with oil of cedar. He decorated the nest with bright flowers and shavings of cedar. Leaving behind some salted meat, Lugalbanda went and hid himself, waiting to see what would happen.

While Lugalbanda fed the chick and decorated the nest, the Anzu Bird was out herding his cattle. When his work was done, he captured one of the bulls and killed it, and he laid it across his back. Then he picked up a live bull in his talons, and with his burdens, he flew home. The Anzu Bird arrived at his nest but could not see his chick inside it. When the Anzu Bird's wife arrived and looked inside the nest, she also saw the chick had gone missing. The Anzu Bird and his wife both sent up a cry of mourning. "Where has our chick gone? Oh, this is a most terrible thing. Who has taken away our precious child?"

The Anzu Bird looked more closely at his nest, and he saw that it had been decorated with bright flowers and cedar shavings, and in the midst of this was the chick, its eyes painted with kohl and its down anointed with oil of cedar. The Anzu Bird saw this and rejoiced. "Look and see! Look what has become of my nest! Surely it is now a palace for a great king. Who has done this? Come, show yourself! Enlil is my father, and I have the power to decide fates and destinies. Show yourself, and I shall make a path for you clear of all enemies and strife!"

Lugalbanda came out from his hiding place and bowed low before the great bird. "O mighty Anzu Bird, your eyes sparkle like a heaven full of stars. Your wingspan is so great the sky can barely encompass it. The sharpness of your talons is beyond compare and is the bane of bulls and cows, sheep and goats. Your feathers are more beautiful than the freshest, most well-tended garden. I came here yesterday, hoping to put myself under your protection; I greet you well and ask that you decide my fate for me."

"Your fate shall be to take away a great gift," said the Anzu Bird. "You will have a great barge full of all good things, grain and cucumbers, apples and gold. That shall be your fate."

"O great Anzu Bird," said Lugalbanda, "that is most generous, but it is not what I desire."

"Take then these arrows," said the bird. "They will always strike their target. You will be the greatest archer in the whole world!"

"O great Anzu Bird," said Lugalbanda, "surely that is a great gift, but it is not what I desire."

"Then take the mighty helmet of Ninurta and his golden breastplate."

"Ah," said Lugalbanda, "you tempt me with great honor, but alas, that is not what I desire."

"What of the butter churn of Dumuzi? It never empties, and it never tires of churning out the sweetest butter," said the bird.

"Indeed that is a fine gift," said Lugalbanda, "but it is not what I desire."

"Now, then, Lugalbanda, it is not good that you should refuse all of my gifts. But I owe you a debt, and so, I will give you whatever you ask of me."

"O great Anzu Bird," said Lugalbanda, "give me the power of running. Let me run and run and never tire! Let me run swift as the lightning, swift as the howling wind. If I look toward the place I wish to go, let me arrive there in no time! Give me this, and I shall command a statue to be made of you, more beautiful than any other statue in the world. All of Sumer shall hear of your beauty and your power, and great praise shall come to you and to the gods thereby."

And so it was that the Anzu Bird gave to Lugalbanda the power of running. He gave to him the power of running without tiring; he gave him the swiftness of the lightning and the howling wind. "And lo," said the bird, "my statue shall be the most beautiful, and my name proclaimed throughout all of Sumer!"

Lugalbanda thanked the bird well for his gift and then asked if the bird knew where his companions were. "I know not," said the bird, "but I will see whether I can find them."

The Anzu Bird spread his great wings and flew aloft. After circling for some time, he spied the troops of Uruk. He returned to his nest and said, "I have found them, Lugalbanda, and I will tell you which way to go, but first you must listen to my words. When you find your companions, do not tell them of the gift I gave you, for one never knows when a gift may turn out to be a curse in disguise. And do not return here to my nest. You stay with your friends."

Lugalbanda took up his weapons and set out to find the troops of the city of Uruk. When he arrived in their camp, they were surprised and happy to see him. "Lugalbanda!" they cried. "Where have you been? We looked for you everywhere but could not find you. We had given you up for dead! No one ever comes back from those mountains alive!"

"Well, I forded the rivers on my own two legs and drank up all their waters," said Lugalbanda. "I ate of what I found in the meadows and of the acorns beneath the trees." All the men of Uruk flocked around Lugalbanda to hear his story, to press food and drink upon him, and to rejoice that he had returned to them unharmed.

The next day, the armies of Uruk marched to the city of Aratta, and they made their encampment outside the walls. The men of Aratta hurled javelins and stones at the men of Uruk. The men of Aratta hurled so many javelins and stones that it was like rain falling from the sky.

For a long time, the men of Uruk fought to take Aratta, but they did not succeed. They tried for many months, and soon the months had turned into a year, and still Aratta did not fall. In front of them, the men of Uruk had a storm of javelins and stones, and behind them they had mountains full of thorns and fell beasts, and no one knew how they might return to their city alive.

King Enmerkar, brave as he was, began to think that maybe this was where he would meet his doom, alongside his army. He asked among his soldiers who would go back to Uruk to find aid, but none would go. He went to his elite soldiers, heroes every one of them, and asked who of them would go to Uruk, but none would go. Again, he asked the regular soldiers, and again, they refused. Once more, Enmerkar went to the elite soldiers and asked who of them would go to Uruk, and this time, Lugalbanda stood forth and said, "O King Enmerkar, I will do this errand, but I must do it alone."

Enmerkar said, "Very well. Go you to Uruk, and go without companions. Take with you the standard of Uruk. Go in haste! Return soon! Guard the standard with your very life!"

Then Enmerkar, son of Utu, said to Lugalbanda, "This is the message you shall bear. Go to my sister Inanna and say: 'O Inanna, my sister! Your wish it was that I raise the city of Uruk from out of the marsh of Uruk. The mighty Enki helped me drain the marsh, and there I built my city, and the building of it took fifty years. And now I find myself here on campaign, and my holy sister has abandoned me. You have fled back to the city of Uruk, leaving me here to lead these armies alone. If you are going to abandon me, at the very least see to it that I return home, so that I might lay aside my spear. And when I return, you may split my shield asunder.' That it what you are to say to my sister Inanna."

Then Lugalbanda left the presence of the king and went to collect what he needed for his journey. Word had spread throughout the camp that Lugalbanda was leaving on the king's errand, and everywhere he went his comrades shouted for him not to leave. "Why must you go?" they said. "Find someone else to do this errand! Do not leave us!"

"I must go," said Lugalbanda. "I made a solemn oath to the king, and I must go alone."

"If you leave you will never return," said his companions. "You must cross those mountains, and no one ever comes down from them alive!"

"I must not tarry," said Lugalbanda. "I must go, and no one must come with me."

Lugalbanda took up his weapons and provisions, and he left the camp. He walked into the mountains and across the plains. He arrived in the city of Uruk by midnight and went before the lady Inanna. Lugalbanda said to her, "O Lady Inanna, greetings. I come to you with a message from your brother, Enmerkar, who bids me say this: 'O Inanna, my sister! Your wish it was that I raise the city of Uruk from out of the marsh of Uruk. The mighty Enki helped me drain the marsh, and there I built my city, and the building of it took fifty years. And now I find myself here on campaign, and my holy sister has abandoned me. You have fled back to the city of Uruk, leaving me here to lead these armies alone. If you are going to abandon me, at the very least see to it that I return home, so that I might lay aside my spear. And when I return, you may split my shield asunder.'"

Inanna listened well to the message of Lugalbanda, and she said to him, "I thank you for bringing me my brother's words. Here is the message you must bring back to him. Tell him that he must go to the holy river of Inanna. On its banks grow the sacred tamarisk trees. One tamarisk stands alone there. Enmerkar must cut down that solitary tamarisk and make from it a bucket. Then he must clean the riverbank of its reeds and catch the holy *suhurmash* fish that swims in those waters. He must cook the fish and season it well, and then he must offer it to the holy war weapon of Inanna. When that is done, Enmerkar shall have the strength he needs to defeat the city of Aratta. And when he has taken the city, he must take from it its metal and metalworkers and its stones and stonemasons. He must rebuild the city and make it his. Enmerkar must do what I command, and then the city of Aratta shall belong to him."

The Sumerian Gilgamesh
Part I: Inanna and the Huluppu Tree

The Sumerian version of the Gilgamesh epic shares certain episodes with the later and more well-known Babylonian version, but other aspects of the Sumerian collection of tales are distinct. The story retold below is one of these distinct myths, telling of events that happened right after the creation of the world. In this story, Gilgamesh is said to be the brother of the goddess Inanna, who has planted a huluppu *tree—possibly a willow, according to Assyriologist Samuel Kramer—from which she wishes to make some furniture. But the female demon Lilith, a serpent, and the Anzu Bird are occupying the tree, preventing Inanna from cutting it down, so she enlists Gilgamesh to help her.*

Although Gilgamesh was an actual historical personage who ruled Sumer some time before circa 2300 BCE, here we see him as a mythologized hero and divine figure who can easily banish such powerful creatures as Anzu Birds and who can uproot whole trees with his bare hands. In gratitude for her brother's help, Inanna uses the branches and roots of the tree to make for Gilgamesh a mikku *and a* pukku, *two objects that are thought to have been the stick and the ball, respectively, that were used in some sort of ancient Sumerian game, the rules of which are now lost.*

Long, long ago, in the first days of the world, in those first days after all had been created by the gods, a *huluppu* tree grew by the banks of the Euphrates River. But one day, a great storm arose, a storm with a great southerly wind, and the wind uprooted the tree and sent it toppling into the water.

The tree floated along down the river. Holy Inanna was walking along the banks of the river, and she saw the tree being carried along by the current. Inanna thought to herself, "If I take this tree home and plant it in my garden in Uruk, it will grow well, and I shall use it to make a fine chair for me to sit upon and a fine couch for me to lie upon."

And so Inanna plucked the tree from the river and then planted it in her garden. Inanna tended the tree well and carefully, waiting for it to grow large enough that she could use it to make her chair and her couch.

After many years, the tree had grown tall, and its trunk had grown thick, and so Inanna thought to cut down the tree, for now it might make a fine chair and a fine couch. But when Inanna tried to cut down the tree, she found that she could not do it. Inanna could not cut down the tree, for a serpent that no magic could touch had twined itself around the trunk at the roots, and the Anzu Bird had made a nest for its young in the branches, and the demon-woman Lilith had made her home inside the trunk.

Inanna saw the serpent and the bird and the woman who had made their homes in her tree, and Inanna wept. She wept many bitter tears, this woman who had known only joy until now. She wept because she could not cut down her tree and make either her fine chair or her fine couch.

Inanna went to her brother, Utu, the god of the sun. She told him all that had happened, how she plucked the tree from the river and planted it in her garden, how she wanted to make a chair and a couch from its wood, but that now she could not cut down the tree because of the serpent and the Anzu Bird and the demon-woman Lilith.

Utu did not listen to his sister. He refused to help Inanna.

Inanna went to her brother, Gilgamesh, the mighty hero. She told him all that had happened, how she plucked the tree from the river and planted it in her garden, how she wanted to make a chair and a couch from its wood, but that now she could not cut down the tree because of the serpent and the Anzu Bird and the demon-woman Lilith.

The mighty Gilgamesh helped his sister, Inanna. Gilgamesh strapped on his armor and took up his mighty axe that he had wielded against many enemies, the armor and the axe that no other man had the strength to bear or wield. Then Gilgamesh summoned his companions from the city of Uruk, and together with his companions, Gilgamesh went to the tree his sister had planted in her garden.

Gilgamesh went to the tree, and he smote the serpent that could not be charmed by magic that had twined itself around the base of the tree. When the Anzu Bird saw what Gilgamesh had done to the serpent, she called to her young, and they all flew away to a far-off land. When the demon-woman Lilith saw what Gilgamesh had done to the serpent, she fled the tree and ran far, far away into the wilderness.

Then Gilgamesh uprooted the tree using nothing but his bare hands and the strength of his arms. Then the companions of Gilgamesh stripped the tree of its branches and tied them neatly into bundles. The trunk of the tree Gilgamesh gave to his sister, Inanna, and from that wood Gilgamesh made her chair and her couch. The roots and the branches of the tree Gilgamesh kept for himself. From the roots, Inanna made for Gilgamesh a *pukku*, and from the branches, she made a *mikku*, the ball and the stick that Gilgamesh used to play his game.

Part II: Enkidu in the Underworld

The greater part of this section of the myth is devoted to a detailed explication of the Sumerian understanding of the afterlife. In the Sumerian Underworld, the fortunate dead are the ones who had many children, especially sons (seven is the perfect number), while those who refused or were unable to produce children become trapped in loops of trivial annoyances. Other fortunate dead are those whose living relatives make offerings to them, as well as the stillborn children, who enjoy a sort of paradise. The lepers, on the other hand, receive no relief from their sufferings, and the warriors killed in battle must exist without comfort, knowing that their loved ones weep for them.

This section of the Sumerian Gilgamesh also varies highly from the Babylonian version in the character of Enkidu. In the Babylonian epic, Enkidu is a hairy wild man sent to kill Gilgamesh but who ends up becoming Gilgamesh's companion in arms and best friend; together, the pair share many heroic adventures. Here in the Sumerian version, however, Enkidu is just as human and just as civilized as his noble master is, and instead of being a heroic figure, he is simply a servant, albeit one whom Gilgamesh loves very deeply.

Gilgamesh took up his *mikku* and *pukku* that he made from the wood of Inanna's *huluppu* tree and then went into the town square and began to play at ball with them. The young men of the town joined him at his game. Together they played, up and down the square. Gilgamesh did not treat the young men kindly. He hit them with the ball; he struck them with his stick. When the widows came to bring food to their sons, the young men complained that Gilgamesh had used them very roughly. When the maidens came to bring water to their brothers, the young men complained that Gilgamesh had hurt them with the violence of his play.

At sunset, Gilgamesh took his stick and marked the last spot where the ball had fallen, thinking to resume the game the next day. He took his stick and ball home, where he had a meal and retired for the night. The next morning, Gilgamesh went back to the town square to play at ball. But the widows and the young maidens had been crying to the gods about how their young men had been treated, and so, Gilgamesh's stick and ball fell out of his hands and went down, down, down into the very Underworld itself.

Gilgamesh tried to get his stick and ball back. Down, down, down he stretched his hand, but he could not reach them. He tried with his foot. Down, down, down he stretched his foot, but he still could not reach his stick and his ball. Gilgamesh went down to the Gate of the Underworld. He sat himself down in front of the gate and began to weep. "Oh, how my heart sorrows for the loss of my stick! Oh, how my eyes weep for the loss of my ball! How will I ever get them back?"

And so it was that Gilgamesh sat before the Gate of the Underworld and mourned the loss of his *mikku* and *pukku*.

Enkidu, the servant of Gilgamesh, heard his master weeping. Enkidu went to Gilgamesh and said, "O my Master, why do you weep so? What has happened that you are in mourning?"

Gilgamesh answered, "My ball and stick have fallen into the Underworld, and I cannot get them back."

"Never fear," said Enkidu. "Weep no more. I will go to the Underworld myself. I will bring back to you your stick and your ball."

"Very well," said Gilgamesh. "Go and fetch them for me. But you must listen to my instructions, and heed them well. Do not wear clean garments. The dead will know you do not belong among them. Do not anoint yourself with oil. The dead will smell the scent and surround you. Do not hurl a throwing stick in the Underworld. Those whom you strike also will surround you. Carry no staff, for that will frighten the spirits and anger them. Neither wear sandals upon your feet, nor speak with a loud voice. Embrace not the wife and son you love. Do not strike a blow upon the wife and son you hate. If they cry out, you will never be allowed to leave!

"The mother of Ninazu is there, the mother of the god of the Underworld. She is a most fearsome creature, one to be avoided, for she wears neither bright garments nor fair linen shifts, and her nails are as long and as sharp as the head of a pickaxe, and she uses these to pluck out her own hair, which grows from her head as leeks grow in a garden!"

But Enkidu did not heed the commands of Gilgamesh. He dressed himself in clean garments and anointed himself with oil. He put his sandals on his feet. He took with him his throwing stick and his staff. And there in the Underworld he hurled the throwing stick and struck some of the dead with it. He spoke with a loud voice. He embraced the wife and son he loved, and he struck the wife and son he hated. Oh, how the cry went up in the Underworld that an intruder was among the spirits of the dead and was using them ill!

Seven days went by. Gilgamesh waited for seven days for his servant Enkidu to return to him, but Enkidu did not return. Gilgamesh began to weep. "Woe, woe, woe! My beloved servant Enkidu has gone into the Underworld and cannot get out."

Gilgamesh went to the E-kur, to the home of the great god Enlil. Gilgamesh knelt before the great Enlil and said, "Woe! My beloved servant Enkidu has gone into the Underworld to fetch me back my *mikku* and *pukku*, but they will not let him out. They will not let him leave the Underworld. Enkidu has ridden through the rage of battle and did not die, yet now he is in the Underworld and cannot leave. He went into the Underworld through its own gate of his own accord. He was not brought there by Namtar, god of fate, or by the demon Asag, or even by Nergal, the god of the Underworld. Enkidu went of his own accord and now cannot leave!"

But Enlil would not hear the prayer of Gilgamesh. Enlil would not release Enkidu from the Underworld.

Next Gilgamesh went to Eridu, the home of the great god Enki. Gilgamesh knelt before the great Enki and said, "Woe! My beloved servant Enkidu has gone into the Underworld to fetch me back my *mikku* and *pukku*, but they will not let him out. They will not let him leave the Underworld. Enkidu has ridden through the rage of battle and did not die, yet now he is in the Underworld and cannot leave. He went into the Underworld through its own gate of his own accord. He was not brought there by Namtar, god of fate, or by the demon Asag, or even by Nergal, the god of the Underworld. Enkidu went of his own accord and now cannot leave!"

Enki listened to the plight of Gilgamesh, and he heard his prayer. Enki turned to his son Utu and said, "You will help Gilgamesh get his servant back. Use your power to make a crack in the Underworld. Bring back Enkidu through this crack."

Utu did what Enki commanded. He caused a great crack to form in the wall of the Underworld. Utu sent a strong wind through the crack. The wind searched out Enkidu and brought him back to the land of the living through the crack Utu had made.

When Enkidu came back to Gilgamesh, Gilgamesh embraced him heartily. Enkidu embraced his master heartily. They both wept tears of joy that Enkidu had come back alive from the Underworld.

"Tell me," said Gilgamesh, "tell me all you saw and heard in the Underworld. Tell me what it is like there, in the land of the dead."

"I can tell you these things," said Enkidu, "but you should sit down first, for surely what I have to tell will make you weep."

"Very well," said Gilgamesh, "I shall sit and weep, only tell me all."

"The organs of generation, the male member and the woman's secret place, are all rotted and turned to dust."

"Oh!" cried Gilgamesh, and then he sat down and began to weep.

"But what of the man who has one son?" said Gilgamesh. "Tell me how it goes with him in the Underworld."

"He looks at the peg that is in the wall next to him, and it makes him weep."

"And the man who has two sons? What of him?"

"He sits on some bricks and eats bread," said Enkidu.

"What of the man who has three sons? How does it go with him?"

"He drinks water that is kept in a waterskin, the sort one hangs on one's saddle," said Enkidu.

Then Gilgamesh asked, "And the man who has four sons, what happens with him in the Underworld?"

"Oh, that man rejoices, just like a man who owns four fine asses to work for him."

"What of the man who has five sons?" asked Gilgamesh.

Enkidu answered, "That man is like a good scribe. He is tireless and always may enter the palace with great ease."

"How does it go with the man who has six sons?"

"That man rejoices as does the farmer who has good land to till," said Enkidu.

"And the man who has seven sons," said Gilgamesh. "How does it go with him?"

"Oh, that man is most blessed," said Enkidu, "for he has leave to sit among the gods and listen to their speech."

"What of the man who has no sons at all?" asked Gilgamesh.

Enkidu replied, "That man must eat bread so hard that it is like a clay tile."

"And the eunuch who serves the king, what of him?"

"He stands in the corner like a useless stick."

"What of the woman who never bore children? How does it go with her?" asked Gilgamesh.

"She is cast aside like an empty pot, and no man ever approaches her."

"And the man who never had relations with his wife," said Gilgamesh. "What of him?"

"He makes a rope, and when it is done, he weeps over it," said Enkidu.

"What of the wife who never had relations with her husband?" asked Gilgamesh.

"She makes a reed mat, and when it is made, she weeps over it."

"And the lepers, how do they fare in the land of the dead?"

"They twitch like oxen do under the sting of flies," said Enkidu.

"What of the warrior who was slain on the field? What becomes of him?"

"His mother cannot comfort him, and his wife weeps without ceasing."

"The dead ones who receive no offerings," said Gilgamesh. "What becomes of them?"

"They live by gleaning crusts of bread thrown into the street by others."

"The little children who are stillborn and have died without even being named, what becomes of them?"

"Oh, they live very well, eating milk and honey off a golden table."

"And the man who was burned to death," said Gilgamesh, "what becomes of him?"

"His spirit is not in the Underworld. It went up into the sky like a wisp of smoke."

Part III: Gilgamesh and Huwawa

Despite his semi-divine nature, Gilgamesh is aware of his own mortality, and here in this story, he wishes to ensure that his name will be known after his death. In his quest to achieve this, he goes to the Mountains of Cedar to cut down trees and there disturbs a powerful and mysterious creature known as Huwawa. Huwawa is not described in the Sumerian version of the myth, but in the Babylonian version—in which he is called Humbaba—he is drawn as a kind of grotesque lion-faced giant whom the god Enlil has charged with protecting the cedar forests.

In this story, Huwawa finds the noise of Gilgamesh's logging activities to be unbearable and thus puts the hero and his companions into an enchanted sleep, which angers Gilgamesh greatly once he awakens and realizes what Huwawa has done. Gilgamesh decides to have his revenge, first by tricking Huwawa into giving Gilgamesh some of his powers. Then Gilgamesh assaults Huwawa and takes him captive, after which Enkidu kills him. In the end, Gilgamesh learns a hard lesson about vengeance and the thirst for power; when Enlil finds out what Gilgamesh and Enkidu have done, he strips Gilgamesh of Huwawa's powers and distributes them throughout the world.

One day, Gilgamesh looked toward the mountains. He looked toward the mountains where the Living One dwelled and thought to himself that he ought to make a journey there. Gilgamesh said to his servant Enkidu, "I have a mind to make a journey to the mountain of the Living One, for death comes to every man regardless of his station. I shall make a journey to that mountain and there shall I establish my name. In places where others have established their names, I also will establish mine. In places where no names have yet been established, I will establish the names of the gods."

Enkidu said, "My lord, a journey to the mountain surely is a good thing, but first you should tell Utu what you purpose to do. Tell Utu, the god of the sun, that you purpose to go to the Mountains of Cedar because all that concerns the mountains concerns Utu. Tell him what you purpose to do."

Gilgamesh saw the wisdom of Enkidu's words, and so, he took up a kid goat and held it to his breast. He took up his sacred staff and held it before his face, and then he spoke to Utu, who dwells in the heavens: "O Utu, O shining one, I purpose to go to the Mountains of Cedar. O Utu, who dwells in the heavens, I am going to the mountains, and I ask your aid!"

Utu replied, "What would you do there in the mountains? In your own land you are a king and a nobleman, but what station would you have in the mountains?"

"O shining one, I have given thought to this. I have given thought to my journey, and I wish you to attend to my thought. I look about my city, and every day people are dying. People die, and then the living mourn them, and all hearts are heavy. I looked over my city wall, I looked at the river, and lo! it was swollen with corpses. I looked over my city wall and saw that, and I know that one day I will be as one of those dead who float in the river. No man may escape his fate, for no man is great enough to achieve this.

"I know that I will die someday. I will die and I will go from this world, but before I do, I wish to establish my name in the mountains. I will establish my name in all places it can be established, and in places where no man's name may be established, I shall establish the names of the gods."

And so it was that Gilgamesh told Utu what he proposed to do, shedding many tears all the while. Utu heard the words of Gilgamesh and saw his tears and accepted those tears as a gift, as one with a compassionate heart always ought to do.

"Let me tell you what I shall do," Utu said to Gilgamesh. "I will help you in your quest. Seven warriors there are, all sons of the same mother. Great and strong are they, one and all! The eldest has a lion's paws and an eagle's talons. The second is a venomous serpent. The third is verily a dragon. The fourth is all made of flame. The fifth is yet another serpent. The sixth is a flood that washes all before him. The seventh is lightning, and none may turn him aside. There is no place on Earth that they do not know, no way or path that is unknown to them, and they will help you on your journey to the Mountains of Cedar."

Gilgamesh rejoiced greatly at the words of Utu. He went into the center of his city and blew a great blast upon his horn. The blast was so great that all who heard it wondered how one man could make such a sound, for it was so loud it sounded as though two men were blowing their horns together with all their might.

Then Gilgamesh said to the people of his city, "I require fifty men to aid me in my quest! Let them be young men and strong, who have not yet married!"

The people followed the commands of Gilgamesh. Fifty young, strong, unmarried men came forward to be the companions of Gilgamesh.

Gilgamesh led the band of fifty to the forge. There he had weapons cast for his men, long knives and battle axes. Then he led his band of fifty to the forest. There they cut down trees of ebony, apricot, and box, and they used the wood for the shafts and hilts of the weapons.

When all was ready, Gilgamesh set out for the mountains. He went to the mountains looking for the perfect cedar tree to use. He crossed the first mountain range, but the perfect cedar was not there. He crossed the second mountain range, but the perfect cedar was not there. He crossed the third mountain range, and the fourth, but the perfect cedar was not there either. He crossed the fifth mountain range, and the sixth, but the perfect cedar was not there. Finally, he came to the seventh mountain range, and there was the perfect cedar, the one Gilgamesh had been seeking.

Gilgamesh took up his mighty axe and felled that great cedar. Enkidu took up his axe and lopped off the branches. The fifty men of Gilgamesh's band picked up the branches and set them neatly in a pile.

The felling of the tree and the lopping and stacking of the branches made a great deal of noise. The noise disturbed Huwawa in his lair. Huwawa was frightened by all the noise, and so, he sent forth his power against Gilgamesh and his men. Suddenly Gilgamesh and his men were overcome with sleep. They all fell to the ground and were insensible.

For a long time they slept, and the first to wake was Enkidu. Enkidu looked about him. He rubbed his eyes and looked about, and everywhere was nothing but silence. Enkidu went to Gilgamesh and touched him, but Gilgamesh did not wake. "O Gilgamesh, O my lord and king, will you yet sleep? Look, the day is nearly ended! Utu is ending his journey and goes to his rest; will you yet sleep? The fifty who came with you, they should go back to their city. Their mothers are waiting for them. Will you yet sleep?"

But Gilgamesh would not wake, so Enkidu took a cloth and soaked it with precious oil. He rubbed the oil over the chest of Gilgamesh, and when this was done, Gilgamesh woke and jumped up on all fours like a great bull. He bent his neck downward and roared, "By the life of Ninsun, the goddess who bore me, and by my father, the great Lugalbanda, how is it that I slumber like a babe, like the babe I was at the breast of Ninsun? I swear that until I find the one who did this to me, I shall not return to my city, and I care not whether that one is mortal or divine!"

Enkidu tried to soothe his master, saying, "My lord, you have not seen the one who did this, but I have! Oh, I have seen him, and he is fearsome to behold. He is a great warrior, with teeth like a dragon. I'll wager he even feasts on man-flesh as do the lions in the desert.

"Go you up into the mountains, but let me return to our city. What shall I tell your mother? Surely she will rejoice if you yet live, but if I must tell her you have died, she will mourn and weep."

"Never fear, Enkidu," said Gilgamesh, "never fear, for we will go together and we will not die, for who will stand against us? Let us go and look for the one who did this. Never fear; let us go and find him!"

But Huwawa never let anyone come nearer to him than sixty pole-lengths, and so fearsome was that creature, that whoever he set his eye upon would die. Huwawa knew that Gilgamesh and Enkidu were approaching, and he said very plainly, "I know you are there! Never shall you return to your city! Never shall you return to your mother!"

Gilgamesh heard the words of Huwawa, and a great wave of terror rose within his body, and he found he could not move. Gilgamesh was filled with fear, and he stood as one rooted to the spot.

Huwawa looked upon Gilgamesh and said, "Look at you, so well made in your body. A beautiful son you are to your mother! A tall tree you are, noble and brave, and the apple of the gods' eyes! Put your hands on the ground, then, don't be afraid!"

Gilgamesh did as Huwawa told him to do, and with his hands on the ground, he said, "By my mother Ninsun, the goddess who bore me, and by my father, the great Lugalbanda! I think you and I should make a pact together. Let me give you my big sister Enmebaragesi to be your wife. Let me also give you my little sister Peshtur to be your concubine! They are yours if you give me your power of fear, and we shall be bound together as kinsmen."

And so, Huwawa gave to Gilgamesh his first power of fear. Gilgamesh's companions took it and stripped off the branches from it. Then they stacked the branches neatly and bound them in bundles and took them all to the foot of the mountain, where they laid them down.

Then Gilgamesh went a second time to Huwawa and said, "By my mother Ninsun, the goddess who bore me, and by my father, the great Lugalbanda! I think you and I should make a pact together. Let me give you *[text lost]*. It is yours if you give me your power of fear, and we shall be bound together as kinsmen."

And so, Huwawa gave to Gilgamesh his second power of fear. The fifty men in Gilgamesh's band lopped off all of its branches. They stacked the branches neatly and bound them in bundles and took them all to the foot of the mountain, where they laid them down.

A third time Gilgamesh went to Huwawa and said, "By my mother Ninsun, the goddess who bore me, and by my father, the great Lugalbanda! I think you and I should make a pact together. Let me give you some of the finest flour there is and the freshest, coolest water in a waterskin. They are yours if you give me your power of fear, and we shall be bound together as kinsmen."

And so, Huwawa gave to Gilgamesh his third power of fear. The fifty men in Gilgamesh's band lopped off all of its branches. They stacked the branches neatly and bound them in bundles and took them all to the foot of the mountain, where they laid them down.

Again, Gilgamesh went to Huwawa and said, "By my mother Ninsun, the goddess who bore me, and by my father, the great Lugalbanda! I think you and I should make a pact together. Here I have some beautiful big sandals for big feet. They are yours if you give me your power of fear, and we shall be bound together as kinsmen."

And so, Huwawa gave to Gilgamesh his fourth power of fear. The fifty men in Gilgamesh's band lopped off all of its branches. They stacked the branches neatly and bound them in bundles and took them all to the foot of the mountain, where they laid them down.

A fifth time Gilgamesh went to Huwawa and said, "By my mother Ninsun, the goddess who bore me, and by my father, the great Lugalbanda! I think you and I should make a pact together. Here I have some beautiful small sandals for small feet. They are yours if you give me your power of fear, and we shall be bound together as kinsmen."

And so, Huwawa gave to Gilgamesh his fifth power of fear. The fifty men in Gilgamesh's band lopped off all of its branches. They stacked the branches neatly and bound them in bundles and took them all to the foot of the mountain, where they laid them down.

Yet again Gilgamesh went to Huwawa and said, "By my mother Ninsun, the goddess who bore me, and by my father, the great Lugalbanda! I think you and I should make a pact together. Here I have some semi-precious stones, chalcedony and lapis lazuli, and some rock crystal besides. They are yours if you give me your power of fear, and we shall be bound together as kinsmen."

And so, Huwawa gave to Gilgamesh his sixth power of fear. The fifty men in Gilgamesh's band lopped off all of its branches. They stacked the branches neatly and bound them in bundles and took them all to the foot of the mountain, where they laid them down.

A seventh time Gilgamesh went to Huwawa. A seventh time Gilgamesh traded goods for Huwawa's power of fear. And so it was that Gilgamesh captured all seven of Huwawa's powers, and each time Gilgamesh took one, he would step a little closer to Huwawa, until he was standing right in front of him. When he was close enough, Gilgamesh made as if to give Huwawa a kiss but instead took his fist and punched Huwawa hard, right in the face, knocking him down.

Huwawa scowled and bared his teeth at Gilgamesh, but before he could rise, Gilgamesh threw a rope about him just as if Huwawa were a wild bull. Gilgamesh tied Huwawa up with the rope.

"You have played me false!" cried Huwawa. "You have tricked me, and you do me wrong by binding me thus!"

Gilgamesh took the end of the rope and dragged Huwawa out of his lair. "Sit down!" said Gilgamesh.

Huwawa sat down and began to weep. He wept and pleaded with Gilgamesh. "Let me go! Oh, please, set me free! Let me speak to Utu, god of the sun! O Utu, O shining one, well you know that I never knew my mother or father. Well you know that I was born here in the mountains and that you were the one who reared me. Well you know that Gilgamesh took an oath to me, swearing by heaven and by Earth and by these mountains."

Huwawa went on his knees before Gilgamesh. He prostrated himself before Gilgamesh, begging for his mercy.

Gilgamesh saw the wretchedness of Huwawa and took pity on him. Gilgamesh turned to Enkidu and said, "Let him go! We should not keep him captive. Let him go!"

But Enkidu replied, "What is this you say, O noble Gilgamesh, my king and my lord? What is this you say, O Gilgamesh, raging bull of battle, beautiful son of your mother? What is this you say, O Gilgamesh, beloved by all the people of your city of Uruk? How is it that you could be so fortunate and so noble and yet understand nothing? If you let him go free, you will never again see your beloved city! If you let him go free, he will see to it that you never return home!"

Then Huwawa said to Enkidu, "Why do you say these things? Why do you speak ill of me to him?"

When Enkidu heard this, he was overcome with rage and cut off Huwawa's head. They put Huwawa's head in a leather bag and went before Enlil with it. They prostrated themselves before Enlil and kissed the ground at his feet then upended the bag so that Huwawa's head spilled out.

Enlil saw the head of Huwawa and was displeased. "Why have you done this thing? You had no orders to kill him. You should have treated him well. You should have shared your bread and your water with him. You should have held him in honor."

Enlil took the seven powers of fear away from Gilgamesh. The first one he gave to the fields. The second one he gave to the rivers. The third went to the reeds in their beds beside the rivers. The lions received the fourth, and the fifth Enlil gave to the forests. The sixth Enlil gave to the palace, and the seventh he gave to Nungal, goddess of prisoners. All the rest of Huwawa's powers of fear Enlil kept for himself.

Part IV: Gilgamesh and Aga

If the wrath of Gilgamesh is on full display in the story of his encounter with Huwawa, here we see his mercy. When Aga, King of Kish, decides to attack Uruk, Gilgamesh defends his city well, as a king ought to do. But of course no army is strong enough to take on Gilgamesh and win, and the outcome of Aga's siege is the defeat of his army and Aga's own captivity. However, Gilgamesh remembers a time when Aga took him in and gave him hospitality, so instead of retribution, Gilgamesh gives Aga his freedom, as repayment for Aga's kindness.

Like Gilgamesh, Aga seems to have been a historical personage. Enmebaragesi, Aga's father, has been identified as an actual King of Kish, suggesting that Aga likely existed as well, and the father and son were the last two kings of the First Dynasty of Kish. (This apparently is not the same Enmebaragesi that Gilgamesh mentions as his sister in the story of Gilgamesh and Huwawa.) Enmebaragesi and Aga seem to have ruled Kish around 2600 BCE, although stories about them entered into the realm of myth sometime after their reigns ended. Kish was located between the Tigris and Euphrates Rivers in what is now central Iraq.

There was a time when Aga, son of Enmebaragesi, was king in Kish, and Gilgamesh, son of Lugalbanda, was king in Uruk. Aga sent his envoys to Uruk, demanding that Gilgamesh submit to him. Gilgamesh called together the elders of the city and the advisors to the king that he might have counsel of them. "We have yet work to be completed here," said Gilgamesh. "There are wells yet to be deepened and others yet to be dug. We should not submit to Kish. Let us bring battle to them instead."

But the elders and advisors all said, "Yes, we have work yet to be completed. We have wells yet to be deepened and others yet to be dug, but this is all the more reason to submit to Kish. We should not bring battle to them."

Gilgamesh was displeased with the words of the elders and advisors, so he went before the men of his city and said, "Envoys from Kish have come and demanded we submit to them. But we have yet work to be completed here. There are wells yet to be deepened and others yet to be dug. Never have we submitted to Kish. So, I ask you, should we bring battle to them instead?"

The men of the city answered, "Who wants to dance attendance on a foreign lord? Surely we do not. We should never submit to Kish! We should bring battle to them instead! Uruk was fashioned by the gods themselves, and Gilgamesh is its king. Gilgamesh is king and warrior, beloved of Father An! The armies of Aga have no hope of victory. They have not enough warriors, and those they do have lack courage. They shall never stand against us."

When Gilgamesh heard the reply of the men of the city, he rejoiced. Gilgamesh went to his servant Enkidu and said, "Make ready for battle! Forge weapons, construct armor! You will take up your mace, and I shall put on my radiant battle gear! Aga stands no chance against us. He will see us and quail, and we will be victorious!"

And so it was that not even five days had passed before Aga brought his armies to Uruk and laid siege to the city, and it went hard with Uruk. Gilgamesh spoke to the warriors of Uruk, saying, "An emissary we must have, someone to go to Aga. Who has the courage?"

Bihartura, one of Gilgamesh's royal guards, spoke up. "I will go! I will go to Aga, and because of me, he will quail before Uruk, and we will be victorious!"

The gate of Uruk was opened, and Bihartura passed through. But he did not get far; the men of Kish were waiting there for him. They captured Bihartura and beat him soundly from head to toe. The men of Kish bound Bihartura and brought him before Aga. Bihartura spoke with the King of Kish, but before he could finish, Aga pointed to the walls of Uruk and said, "Who is that there on the ramparts? Is that your king?"

Bihartura looked and saw that one of the officers of the army of Uruk was on the ramparts.

"That is not my king," said Bihartura. "If it were my king, you would know it. If it were my king, you would quail in fear before him. If it were my king, a multitude would fall before him and yet another multitude arise to greet him. If it were my king, all nations would bow before him, and Aga, King of Kish, would be bound and brought before him as a captive."

At these words, the men of Kish beat Bihartura again from head to toe. While they were thus beating him, Gilgamesh went to the top of the walls of Uruk and stood upon the rampart. All in the city who saw him marveled at his glory. Gilgamesh ordered that the men of the city be given maces, and then he placed them at the ready behind the city gate. The gate opened, but Gilgamesh held the men back, sending Enkidu through the gate alone.

In the camp of Kish, Aga saw Gilgamesh upon the ramparts, and he said to Bihartura, "Is that man your king?"

"Yes," said Bihartura, "that is my king."

And so it was that what Bihartura had said of Gilgamesh came true. A multitude fell before him while yet another multitude rose up to greet him. The nations bowed before him, and Aga, King of Kish, was bound and brought before Gilgamesh as a captive.

Gilgamesh looked upon Aga and said, "You treated me with kindness when I was in need. You took me in and kept me safe when I was a fugitive. I therefore repay that debt, here in the sight of Utu." And with that, Gilgamesh set Aga free to return to his own country.

When the army of Uruk saw the way Gilgamesh treated Aga, they cried out, "Praise to the lord of Uruk! Praise to the one who keeps fast the walls built by An himself!"

Sargon and Ur-Zababa

Unlike Lugalbanda and Enmerkar, who cannot be proven to have been actual kings of Sumer, Sargon of Akkad was a historical personage and the founder of the first empire in Mesopotamia, often called the Akkadian Empire. Sargon's exploits are well attested in history, but he also became the subject of legends. One such legend has to do with the mystery of his origins: like the biblical Moses, Sargon supposedly was set adrift on a river in a basket of rushes and then raised as a son by the man who found him.

Among Sargon's conquests was the land of Sumer, and so tales about Sargon exist in Sumerian as well as Akkadian sources. The Sumerian story retold below explains Sargon's initial rise to power as the successor to Ur-Zababa, who was King of Kish, a Sumerian city-state located between the Tigris and Euphrates Rivers in what is now central Iraq. In this tale, Sargon has already achieved the high status of cupbearer to the king. But the fall of Ur-Zababa has already been decided by the gods, An and Enlil, and so Sargon receives divine assistance from the goddess Inanna in his rise to power. As such, this story is part of a greater ancient tradition of mythography as a tool of propaganda legitimizing a leader's rule.

One important part of the story's plot has to do with Ur-Zababa's attempt to get rid of Sargon by sending him to a blacksmith on an errand that is supposed to lead to Sargon's demise. The means by which Sargon was to be killed is not immediately clear to modern readers; in the collection of Sumerian literature translated by Assyriologist Jeremy Black and others, Ur-Zababa orders that Sargon and a bronze mirror are to be thrown "into the mould [sic] *like statues." I have taken that description to indicate that Sargon was to have been put into a mold used to cast bronze and then killed by having molten metal poured on top of him.*

The great city of Kish was ruled by Ur-Zababa. A beautiful city was Kish, and a prosperous one, surrounded by fertile fields watered by many well-tended canals. But the reign of Ur-Zababa was about to come to a close, for An and Enlil had decreed that he should no longer rule over the city.

One of the workers at the royal palace of Kish was a man named Sargon. His duty was to oversee deliveries of goods to the palace. He did his duties thoroughly and well, so well, in fact, that the king appointed Sargon as the royal cupbearer, a position of great trust and importance.

There came a time when Ur-Zababa went to his rest. He slept in his royal bed, and while he was sleeping, he had a dream. When he woke, he understood what the dream was about. It troubled him, but he did not tell anyone about it. Five days passed after the dream, but not more than ten, and King Ur-Zababa became frightened and unwell. He became afflicted with a disease of the bladder. He could not contain his urine, and what passed had blood and pus in it.

While Ur-Zababa was thus afflicted, Sargon went to his bed one night, and he also had a dream. He dreamed of the goddess Inanna. In Sargon's dream, the goddess took King Ur-Zababa and drowned him in a river of blood. The goddess said to Sargon, "I am doing this for you." It was a terrifying dream, and Sargon writhed and groaned in his sleep.

Other people in the palace heard Sargon's groans, and they told the king about them. The king then called Sargon into his presence and said, "Why were you groaning in the night?"

"I was having a bad dream, O mighty Ur-Zababa," said Sargon.

"Tell me of this dream," said the king.

"As you wish, my king," said Sargon. "I dreamed of a young woman. She was the most beautiful I had ever seen. She was so tall her head reached to the heavens. She was so strong she was like the great wall of a city, broad and immovable. The woman drowned you in a river of blood. She told me she did that for me."

Ur-Zababa heard the dream of Sargon and became even more frightened than before. He crafted a plan to rid himself of Sargon. First, he called to himself Belishtikal, the chief smith. Ur-Zababa said to the smith, "That cupbearer of mine has had a dream of ill omen. He dreamed that the lady Inanna drowned me in a river of blood. I want to rid myself of Sargon. I shall send him to your smithy on an errand. I shall give him my bronze mirror and tell him to take it to you at your smithy in the E-sikil, the House of Purity, to be repaired. When Sargon arrives, throw him and the mirror alike into a mold for casting bronze. Pour molten bronze on top of them. Make a statue of it. Then no one shall be the wiser about the death of the cupbearer."

Belishtikal returned to the E-sikil and made the mold as the king had commanded him. Then Ur-Zababa called Sargon to him. He handed Sargon the small bronze mirror and said, "Take this to the smith Belishtikal at the E-sikil. It needs to be repaired."

Sargon took the mirror and left the palace to do the king's bidding. But on the way to the E-sikil, the goddess Inanna appeared to him and blocked his way. "You must not go into the E-sikil! The E-sikil is the House of Purity, and you are stained by blood! Do not enter that House!"

And so it was that when Sargon arrived at the E-sikil, he would not enter but rather waited at the gate for the smith to come to him. Sargon delivered the mirror and returned to the palace unharmed. He resumed his duties as cupbearer, and the king said nothing to him of what the errand to the smith was intended to accomplish.

Five days passed, but not more than ten, and again, King Ur-Zababa had a frightening dream. He understood what it foretold, but he did not tell anyone else about it.

Now, in the days of Ur-Zababa, writing had been invented for some time. Scribes would write with a stylus on soft clay, and when the clay was dry, the tablet could be stored or delivered. It was common for people to exchange writings in this way, but as of yet, they did not put the tablets inside envelopes. One day, Ur-Zababa sent Sargon on a mission to deliver a tablet of writing to Lugalzagesi, the King of Uruk. The message on the tablet asked Lugalzagesi to kill Sargon.

[Here the story breaks off, and the few lines about Lugalzagesi that remain are fragmented. Presumably the rest of the story would have told us how Sargon evaded being murdered a second time and how he came to take Ur-Zababa's throne and thus begin the foundation of his empire.]

Check out more mythology books by Matt Clayton

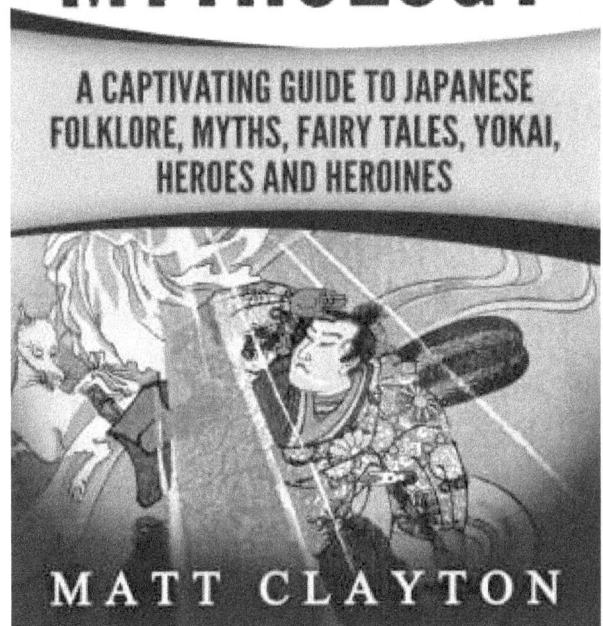

Bibliography

Barton, George A. *Miscellaneous Babylonian Inscriptions.* New Haven: Yale University Press, 1918.

Black, Jeremy et al. *The Literature of Ancient Sumer.* Oxford: Oxford University Press, 2004.

——— *The Electronic Text Corpus of Sumerian Literature* (http://www-etcsl.orient.ox.ac.uk/), Oxford 1998- .

Cohen, Sol. *Enmerkar and the Lord of Aratta.* PhD Dissertation. University of Pennsylvania. 1973.

Cooper, Jerrold S., and Wolfgang Heimpel. "The Sumerian Sargon Legend." *Journal of the American Oriental Society* 103/1 (1983): 67-82.

Echlin, Kim. *Inanna: A New English Version.* Toronto: Penguin Books, 2015.

Gadotti, Alhena. *Gilgamesh, Enkidu, and the Netherworld and the Sumerian Gilgamesh Cycle.* Boston: De Gruyter, Inc., 2014.

George, Andrew, trans. *The Epic of Gilgamesh: The Babylonian Epic Poem and Other Texts in Akkadian and Sumerian.* London: Penguin Books, Ltd., 2000.

Hallo, William W., ed. *The Context of Scripture: Canonical Compositions, Monumental Inscriptions, and Archival Documents from the Biblical World.* 3 Vols. Boston: Brill, 2003.

Hooke, Samuel Henry. *Middle Eastern Mythology.* Baltimore: Penguin Books, 1963.

Kramer, Samuel Noah. "The Sumerian Deluge Myth: Reviewed and Revised." *Anatolian Studies* 33 (1983): 115-121.

———. "Interim Report on Work at the Museum at Istanbul." *Bulletin of the American Schools of Oriental Research* 104 (1946): 8-12.

———. *Sumerian Mythology: A Study of Spiritual and Literary Achievement in the Third Millennium B. C.* Philadelphia: The American Philosophical Society, 1944.

———. *Gilgamesh and the* Huluppu-*Tree: A Reconstructed Sumerian Text.* Chicago: University of Chicago Press, 1938.

Lambert, W. G. *Babylonian Creation Myths.* Winona Lake: Eisenbrauns, 2013.

Langdon, Stephen Herbert. *Mythology of All Races.* Vol. 5: *Semitic.* New York: Cooper Square Publishers, 1964.

———. *Sumerian Epic of Paradise, the Flood, and the Fall of Man.* Philadelphia: University of Pennsylvania University Museum, 1915.

Leeming, David Adams. *The World of Myth: An Anthology.* Oxford: Oxford University Press, 1990.

Leick, Gwendolyn. *Sex and Eroticism in Mesopotamian Literature.* London: Routledge, 1994.

———. *A Dictionary of Ancient Near Eastern Mythology*. London: Routledge, 1991.

Mark, Joshua J. "Sargon of Akkad." *Ancient History Encyclopedia*, 2 September 2009. https://www.ancient.eu/Sargon_of_Akkad/.

Meador, Betty De Shong. *Inanna, Lady of Largest Heart: Poems of the Sumerian High Priestess Enheduanna*. Austin: University of Texas Press, 2000.

Pritchard, James B., ed. *Ancient Near Eastern Texts Relating to the Old Testament*. 3rd ed. Princeton: Princeton University Press, 1969.

Wolkstein, Diane, and Samuel Noah Kramer. *Inanna, Queen of Heaven and Earth: Her Stories and Hymns from Sumer*. New York: Harper & Row, 1983.

Glossary

Abu	God created by **Ninhursag**
Adgarkidu	Daughter of the god **Numushda** and the goddess **Namrat**; wife of the god **Martu**
Aga	King of the city-state of **Kish**; ruled c. 2600 BCE
Amorites	Ancient nomadic people from what is now Syria
An	God of the sky; supreme Sumerian deity; son of Apsu and Namma; one of the **Annunaki**
Annunaki	The greater or elder gods
Anzu Bird	Mythical lion-headed bird creature
Apsu, the	Dwelling-place of **Enki**; also refers to both groundwater and the freshwater marshes of Sumer
Aratta	Mythical city that was very wealthy; rival to **Uruk** and **Kulaba**

Aruru	Another name for **Ninhursag**
Asag, the	Monstrous demon-creature defeated by **Ninurta**
Azimua	Goddess created by **Ninhursag**; wife of **Ningishzida**
Babylon	Ancient Mesopotamian city in what is now Iraq
Bau	Goddess of healing and consort of **Ninurta**
Belishtikal	Bronze-smith in the story of **Sargon** and **Ur-Zababa**
Bihartura	Soldier in the army of **Gilgamesh**
Dilmun	In Sumerian myth, a type of earthly paradise; in actuality was a region and culture on the eastern edge of the Arabian Peninsula along the Persian Gulf
Dumuzi	Shepherd-god who becomes the husband of **Inanna**
E-kur	Mythical house of the god **Enlil** in **Nippur**; also refers to the physical temple built by the Sumerians for the worship of Enlil

E-sikil	Temple mentioned in the story of **Sargon** and **Ur-Zababa**
Ebih	Mountain in the Zagros Range; in myth it refuses to bend the knee to **Inanna** and is punished for it
Elam	Ancient country on the northeastern shore of the Persian Gulf in what is now Iran
Enbilulu	God of canals; son of **Enlil** and **Ninlil**
Enegir	City mentioned in the myth of the journey of **Nanna** to **Nippur**
Enheduanna	Daughter of **Sargon of Akkad**, high priestess of **Inanna** and **Nanna** in **Ur**, first named author in history
Enki	"Lord Earth"; creator god and trickster, primarily associated with water; lives in the **Apsu**; son of Apsu and Namma; one of the **Annunaki**
Enkidu	Companion and servant of **Gilgamesh**
Enkimdu	One of several Sumerian

	agricultural gods
Enlil	"Lord Air"; chief god of the Sumerian pantheon; lives in the **E-kur**; one of the **Annunaki**
Enmebaragesi (i)	Sister of **Gilgamesh**
Enmebaragesi (ii)	Historical king of the city-state of **Kish** and father of **Aga**
Enmerkar	Pseudo-historical king of **Uruk**; supposed father of **Lugalbanda**; supposed grandfather of **Gilgamesh**
Enshagag	God created by **Ninhursag**; given **Dilmun** as his domain
Ensuhkeshdanna	Mythical king of the city-state of **Aratta**; rival to **Enmerkar**
Ereshkigal	Goddess of the Underworld
Gilgamesh	Mythical hero; likely based on a historical Sumerian king who became deified and mythologized; supposed son of **Lugalbanda** and grandson of **Enmerkar**
Hamazu	Place mentioned as home of the sorcerer **Urgirinuna** in the story of **Enmerkar** and **Ensuhkeshdanna**

Huluppu Tree	Mythical tree rescued from a river by **Inanna**; possibly a willow tree
Huwawa	Mythical being sent to guard the **Mountain of Cedar** by **Enlil**; captured by **Gilgamesh** and slain by **Enkidu**
Id-kura	The river that separates the land of the living from the Underworld
Igigi	The lesser or younger gods
Inab	City mentioned in the story of the marriage of **Martu**
Inanna	Goddess of fertility, procreation, and war; often identified with the planet Venus; one of the **Annunaki**
Isimud	Adviser to **Enki**
Kalkal	Gatekeeper of the **E-kur** in **Nippur**
Ki-ur	Place mentioned in the myth of **Enlil** and **Ninlil**
Kish	Ancient Mesopotamian city between the Tigris and Euphrates Rivers in what is now Iraq

Kulaba	Another name for **Uruk**
Larsa	City mentioned in the story of the journey of **Nanna** to **Nippur**
Lilith	A demon-woman who inhabits the **huluppu tree**
Lugalbanda	Pseudo-historical king of **Uruk** and mythical hero; supposed father of **Gilgamesh** and son of **Enmerkar**
Lugalzagesi	Last king of Sumer before the conquest of **Sargon of Akkad**
Lulubi Mountains	Part of the Zagros range, now on the border between Iraq and Iran
Magan	Place mentioned in the story of **Enki** and **Ninhursag**; may have referred to Upper Egypt
Martu	God who represents the **Amorite** people
mikku	Stick used in an ancient Sumerian ball game
Mountains of Cedar	Mythical place where the creature **Huwawa** lives
Namma	Mother goddess; wife and mother of **An**; mother of **Enki**

Namrat	Wife of the god **Numushda**
Namtar	God of fate; vizier to **Ereshkigal**
Nanna	God of the moon; son of **Enlil** and **Ninlil**; one of the **Annunaki**
Nazi	Goddess of justice and commerce; daughter of **Ninhursag** and **Enki**
Nergal	God of war; consort of **Ereshkigal**; son of **Enlil** and **Ninlil**
Ninazu	"Lord Healer"; son of **Enlil** and **Ninlil**; god of boundaries
Ningirida	Goddess of **Enegir**
Ningishzida	"Lord of the Good Tree"; god associated with the Underworld
Ninhursag	"Lady of the Wild Hills"; creator goddess and consort of **Enki**; one of the **Annunaki**
Ninkasi	Goddess who fulfills wishes
Ninkura	"Lady of the Land"; daughter of **Enki** and **Ninsar**
Ninlil	"Lady Air"; consort of **Enlil**;

	mother of **Nanna**, **Nergal**, **Enbilulu**, and **Ninazu**
Ninmah	Another name for **Ninhursag**
Ninsar	Daughter of **Enki** and **Ninhursag**
Ninsikila	"Lady of Purity"; daughter of **Enki**; associated with **Dilmun** in the story of **Enki** and **Ninhursag**
Ninsun	"Lady of the Wild Cows"; mother of **Gilgamesh** and wife of **Lugalbanda**
Ninsutu	Goddess created by **Ninhursag**; consort of **Ninazu**
Ninti	Goddess created by **Ninhursag**; associated with calendars
Nintul	God created by **Ninhursag**; lord of **Magan**
Ninunuga	Goddess of **Shuruppag**
Ninurta	Hero-god of agriculture; associated with legal judgement; son of **Enlil** and **Ninhursag**; slayer of the **Asag** and bearer of the **Sharur**
Nippur	City in ancient Sumer between

	the Tigris and Euphrates Rivers in what is now Iraq
Nisaba	Goddess associated with grain; also seen as a patroness of scribes
Numushda	God mentioned in the story of the marriage of **Martu**; father of **Adgarkidu** and consort of **Namrat**
Nunbarshegunu	Mother of **Ninlil**
Nuska	Adviser to **Enlil**; titled "Master Builder of the E-kur" in the story of Enlil and **Ninlil**
Peshtur	Sister of **Gilgamesh**
pukku	Ball used for an ancient Sumerian game
Rimush	Brother of **Enheduanna**
Sagburu	A "wise woman" of **Uruk** who defeats the sorcerer **Urgirinuna**
Sargon of Akkad	Historical king and creator of the Akkadian Empire
Seven, the	Divine warriors each having different attributes
Sharur, the	The sentient battle mace

	belonging to **Ninurta**
Sherida	Goddess mentioned in the story of the journey of **Nanna** to **Nippur**; consort of **Utu**
Shuruppag	City in ancient Sumer mentioned in the story of the journey of **Nanna** to **Nippur**
Sin	Another name for **Nanna**
Subir	Region in Upper Mesopotamia
Suen	Another name for **Nanna**
Tummal	City in ancient Sumer mentioned in the story of the journey of **Nanna** to **Nippur**
Umul	Creature created by **Enki** in his contest with **Ninmah**; either a severely disabled adult or the first baby
Ur	Ancient Sumerian city on the south bank of the Euphrates in what is now Iraq
Ur-Zababa	King of **Kish**
Urgirinuna	Sorcerer who tries to help **Ensuhkeshdanna** win his contest with **Enmerkar**
Uruk	Ancient Sumerian city; home to **Enmerkar, Lugalbanda,**

	and **Gilgamesh**; rival to **Aratta**
Uttu	Goddess of weaving; daughter of **Enki** and **Ninkura**
Utu	God of the sun
Zabu Mountains	Ancient name for the Zagros Mountains, which run across the southern part of Turkey and then turn southeast to run between Iran and Iraq and from there along the eastern shore of the Persian Gulf
Zangara	God of dreams

Translations of names taken from Gwendolyn Leick, A Dictionary of Ancient Near Eastern Mythology *(London: Routledge, 1991).*

www.ingramcontent.com/pod-product-compliance
Lightning Source LLC
Chambersburg PA
CBHW070048230426
43661CB00005B/818